AND THE TEARS
FLOWED

William L. McCarron

Copyright © 2024 William L. McCarron.

All rights reserved. No part of this book may be reproduced, stored, or transmitted by any means—whether auditory, graphic, mechanical, or electronic—without written permission of both publisher and author, except in the case of brief excerpts used in critical articles and reviews. Unauthorized reproduction of any part of this work is illegal and is punishable by law.

ISBN: 979-8-89419-485-1 (sc)
ISBN: 979-8-89419-487-5 (hc)
ISBN: 979-8-89419-488-2 (e)

Because of the dynamic nature of the Internet, any web addresses or links contained in this book may have changed since publication and may no longer be valid. The views expressed in this work are solely those of the author and do not necessarily reflect the views of the publisher, and the publisher hereby disclaims any responsibility for them.

One Galleria Blvd., Suite 1900, Metairie, LA 70001
(504) 702-6708

CONTENTS

List of Figures/Maps v
Acknowledgements vii
Introduction ix

Chapter 1   The Beginning – Enlistment,
            Basic Training, and Infantry OCS 1
Chapter 2   Airborne, Ranger, and Fort Ord 6
Chapter 3   Departure, Arrival, and Assignment 10
Chapter 4   In Country Assignment 14
Chapter 5   Introduction and Assignment to the 1/8th 17
Chapter 6   Introduction to B Company 1/8th Cavalry (ABN) 20
Chapter 7   Operation Lincoln 28
Chapter 8   Base Camp and Highway 19 Security 36
Chapter 9   Operation Crazy Horse – Into Battle 44
Chapter 10 Crazy Horse - Movement to Contact 49
Chapter 11 Crazy Horse - Contact 61
Chapter 12 Crazy Horse -The Assault 68
Chapter 13 Crazy Horse – Consolidation and Clean Up 72
Chapter 14 Crazy Horse – The Aftermath 77
Chapter 15 Crazy Horse – LZ Colt and Change of Command 79
Chapter 16 Back to the Mountains 82
Chapter 17 Base Camp and Stand Down 86
Chapter 18 Kontum, RVN 91
Chapter 19 Evacuation to Camp Zama, Japan 94
Chapter 20 Zama – And a Girl Named Miyoka 99

Chapter 21	Farewell, Back into the Breech, and Nathan Hale	104
Chapter 22	Operation Thayer 1 and LZ Hammond	115
Chapter 23	Villaronga Takes Charge	124
Chapter 24	Phan Thiet/Task Force Byrd and Back to Japan	130
Chapter 25	Operation Pershing, LZ Gavin, and the Battle of the 506 Valley	137
Chapter 26	Christmas Cease Fire and LZ Bird	147
Chapter 27	Battle of Gia Duc	150
Chapter 28	Graves Registration and Operation Thayer II	164
Chapter 29	Familiar Territory or Was It	168
Chapter 30	The Rock	171
Chapter 31	Continued Operations and the Move to LZ English	174
Chapter 32	LZ Sand and the Bong Song Plain	177
Chapter 33	Two Idiots	183
Chapter 34	Conclusion	185

In Memorium 187
Glossary of Terms 201

LIST OF FIGURES/MAPS

Fig 1. Lt Col Levin Broughton
Fig 2. Lt Col Kenneth Mertel
Fig 3. Captain Roy Martin
Fig 4. 1SGT Ray Poynter
Fig 5. 2nd Lt Bill Hughes
Fig 6. 2nd LT Robert Crum
Fig 7. 1st Lt Jack Peevy
Fig 8. PSG James Johnson
Fig 9. LT Roger Talmadge
Fig 10. SP4 Adell Alston
Fig 11. MG John Norton
Fig 12. Denver Trail, LZ Hereford, LZ Horse, Battle Area
Fig 13. Captain William Mozey
Fig 14. Movement to Battle
Fig 15. Parks Wounded
Fig 16. Lunch/CPTs Martin and Mozey
Fig 17. Hand Drawn Map of Battle
Fig 18. SGT Gerald Hoover
Fig 19. Assault on Enemy Position
Fig 20. 1st Lt Frank Varek
Fig 21. PFC Alan Ritter
Fig 22. PFC David Dolby
Fig 23. Captain Gerrell V Plummer
Fig 24. SSGT Bobby James
Fig 25. SP4 Johnny Hickey
Fig 26. SSGT Charles Edwards
Fig 27. MG Stanley Larsen
Fig 28. SP4 Charles Allen
Fig 29. BG William Becker

Fig 30. 1SGT Robert Craig
Fig 31. SSGT Bill Odom and 1st SGT Bob Craig
Fig 32. Captain Raul (Roy) Villaronga
Fig 33. Gia Duc (1)
Fig 34. LZ Betty and Virginia
Fig 35. Phan Thiet: Myself, the CO, Platoon Leaders, and FO
Fig 36. LtCol Ardie McClure
Fig 37. Air Assault LZ Gavin
Fig 38. SP5 Maurice Waters and CO tend to PFC Jesse Smith
Fig 39. Sp5 Waters, CPT Villaronga and Sp4 Lloyd Jack Tend to U/I Soldier
Fig 40. Map: Area of 506 Battle
Fig 41. PFC Mark English
Fig 42. SP4 Pat O'Brien, Mark English LZ Hammond
Fig 43. SP4 Robert Carter
Fig 44. Movement to Contact Gia Duc (!)
Fig 45. Platoon Positions Prior to the Attack on Gia Duc(1)
Fig 46. Attack on Gia Duc
Fig 47. SP4 Erineo (Ernie) Mendez
Fig 48. SGT Jerry Diersing
Fig 49. PFC Walter Wonnacott, Medic
Fig 50. 1st Lt Lamont Finch, Platoon leader, 4th Platoon
Fig 51. PSG Lonnie Barber, 4th Platoon
Fig 52. Sp4 Dennis Spahn, PFC James Pawlak
Fig 53. 1st Lt Daniel Hennessy, Platoon Leader 1st Platoon
Fig 54. SP4 Eric Brannfors, Sp4 Carl Mercer, CPL Doug Hoag, PFC Richard Jacobs
Fig 55. Captain John Titus, CO, A Company, 1/8th
Fig 56. SGT Daniel Herrando, Artillery Recon Sergeant, 2/19th Artillery
Fig 57. Lt Roger Riffle, Platoon Leader, 3rd Platoon
Fig 58. LZ Sand
Fig 59. Connie and I, Fort Benning, 1967

ACKNOWLEDGEMENTS

In writing and publishing this book I want to acknowledge a number of people who were instrumental in assisting my efforts. In particular, I would like to recognize Katie Dahm, Erin Mitchell, Savannah Parker and the editorial staff of Palmetto Publishing who have assisted me through the long and sometimes arduous task of publishing my first book. They have been tremendous and helpful in leading me through the process. A special thanks also to Shirley Stiers, a dear friend, who reviewed, the initial manuscript suggesting grammatical corrections as well as insightful recommendations to improve the original draft. Thanks also to my brother and hero John Wallace McCarron, who reviewed the book over a two day period while undergoing the rigors of cancer treatments, pneumonia, and several other medical problems, but still found time to encourage me "go for it." Similarly, I cannot forget to thank my wife of 50 years Connie Russell McCarron, who through our years of marriage encouraged me to sit down and put my recollections to paper. Thank you "Babycakes" for all the wonderful memories. I love and miss you. Also for the support of my sons; Lonnie, Randy, and Russ. In a like manner I cannot forget to acknowledge my current companion, Mary Jo, who has sat through countless hours while I typed on my computer putting thoughts and memories to paper. She has been fantastic and supportive at all times. Last, but not least, my thoughts of my fellow brothers; those soldiers who served with me during our tour in Vietnam, and who I thank for the memories, encouragement and friendship we share to this day. Honor and Courage.

INTRODUCTION

May 21, 1966 a day myself and others of Bravo Company, 1st Battalion, 8th Cavalry (ABN) will not soon forget as we entered into one of the most intense and violent small arms infantry battles of the Vietnam War. It lasted more than 5 hours and was fought by an undermanned US rifle company against a strongly reinforced enemy battalion; the 8th Battalion, 22nd NVA Regiment, Sao Pang Division, reinforced by a VC heavy weapons Company containing at least two 50 caliber machine guns and three 30 caliber machine guns on a field of their choosing.

The US Company was led by Captain Roy Martin, a tough, courageous and proud man of the storied 1st Battalion (Airborne), 1st Brigade (Airborne) 1st Cavalry Division, one of the most decorated units to serve in the Vietnam conflict from 1965 until final withdrawal of all combat troops in 1973. We were supported in the battle by our sister unit, C Company 1/8th, who controlled the high ground to our north, and who placed heavy suppressive fires on the fortified NVA positions to our south.

We were proud, tough Airborne Soldiers and feared no man or unit as we prepared to go into battle with one of the toughest adversaries the world has ever known. I should know as I was one of many proud ground force leaders and infantrymen who fought them continuously from the time the 1st Cavalry Division arrived in Vietnam until their final withdrawal in 1973.

This is an accounting of my one year tour in Vietnam. It begins with my enlistment in the US Army, Basic Training, Officer Candidate School, duty at Fort Ord, California and then arrival at Tan Son Nhut Airport, Republic of Vietnam in March 1966 and basically ends with my departure in March 1967 a survivor in body only, but with mental scars that endure to this day. With the grace of God and the eternal love and support of my wife until her death in 2017, I now commit to relating my one year as an infantry officer in Vietnam.

CHAPTER 1

THE BEGINNING – ENLISTMENT, BASIC TRAINING, AND INFANTRY OCS

I entered the Army on March 31, 1964 and after being sworn in at Richmond, Virginia was provided orders and a train ticket to report along with a number of other recruits to Ft Jackson, South Carolina for Basic Training. Basic Training was an eight week course designed to teach us the fundamentals of Army life from drill and ceremonies, to maintaining individual and company equipment, and most importantly learning how to become soldiers. The drill sergeants responsible for our training were Korean War veterans and some also had served in WWII. They were dedicated to taking raw recruits who knew nothing about the Army and turning them into well trained soldiers. Under the tutelage of steely eyed M/SGT Charles Linn, the Senior Field NCO, and each of the platoon drill instructors that led us through the process they themselves had accomplished years before. We were taught drill and ceremonies, physical training, hand to hand combat, bayonet training, and first aid the first two weeks of training. Weapons and grenade training followed along with map reading and land navigation and all the other soldierly skills needed to become a soldier. The culmination of the eight week training ended with bivouac and then a twelve mile march back to garrison. Linn and the other drill instructors were tough on us but fair. Following a formal parade and graduation each of the DI's congratulated us on our successful completion of Basic Training and wished us well in our future Army endeavors as we moved on to further Military Occupational Training or assignment to a regular Army unit.

Following Basic, I along with two others graduates, were ordered to report to Fort Benning, Georgia to attend The Infantry Officers Candidate School (OCS) under a program called the College Option Program. I had completed all the standard tests for admission as well as all the physical tests while in my junior/senior year of college. OCS was a six month course designed to mold former enlisted soldiers and recent college graduates into brand new Infantry 2nd Lieutenants. Ft Sill, Oklahoma (Artillery); Fort Knox, Kentucky (Armor); and Ft Belvoir, Virginia (Engineers) had also established similar courses for their branch of arms.

I arrived a week before the class start in June 1964 and was warmly welcomed by the cadre of the 51st Company (OCS), 5th Student Battalion, who had the responsibility to turn us into officers as best they could or to send those that didn't fit the bill back to their former unit of assignment or to a new assignment as enlisted men to serve out the remainder of their terms of service. I was soon to find out this warm welcome would turn into hell as the remainder of class 10-64 reported for training. Each OCS Company in the 5th Student Battalion had a Company Commander, a Captain of Infantry; a 1st Sergeant, a Company Clerk and a Supply Sergeant. The company also had a Tactical Officers (TACs), 1st or 2nd Lieutenants assigned to each platoon in the company to mentor their OC students and sergeants to assist the TACs with the training. The building housing the candidates were three storied brick buildings, the bottom floor housed offices for the cadre, the company orderly room, the mess hall and supply room. The second and third floors were rooms for the students with a large community latrine in the center of each floor for student use. Two platoons were housed on each of these floors. Life was easy for me this first week, but that was about to change.

On the following Sunday candidates started reporting to the Company. I was appointed as a guide to meet and direct the candidates to the back of the building and through the double doors into the mess hall for them to begin in-processing. It was here where all hell broke loose. TAC officers and NCOs were screaming out orders so fast candidates didn't know which way to turn. Drop and give me ten, get outside and report properly, why are you smiling at me, drop and give me ten, get out and report properly, etc. Reporting in began at noon and some of the candidates didn't make it to their assigned space within the building until 2300 Hours; disheveled, exhausted, and shell shocked from their initial meeting with the dreaded TAC Officers.

Reporting into the Company ended at 1700 hours and after showing the last of the new candidates where to go it then became my turn. All the comradery shown to me the first week quickly vanished as the TACS descended on me with a vengeance. I have never done so many pushups and sit ups in my life or at least so it seemed. This was the pace we would lead for most of the next 24 weeks, albeit things did begin to approve after the eighteenth week. Run everywhere with TACs screaming all the time. The normal day started at 0430 hours with Physical Training followed by showers and shaves. Everything regimented. Pull ups to enter the dining hall. Rush through the mess line and take what was put on your tray, move to a table that seated eight; wait until all reached the table, then sit on command. Each man sat on the front portion of the chair and then squared the meal, meaning lift the food straight up from the plate and then bring it straight back and into your mouth while looking straight ahead. You then squared it back to the plate for the next bite of food, all the time the TACS screaming in your ear or trying to make you laugh so they could drop you for the dreaded 10 pushups, time and time again. Seldom did you finish your meal before they were yelling to get out of their dining facility. Hunger was a common virtue.

Everything was spit shined including the floors in the hallways and your shared rooms and everything had a proper place for display. Each candidate had one footlocker, one wall locker, and one dresser. The foot locker was for you to maintain your own private items, as long as you kept it locked. God forbid if you failed to do this. Should it happen you could expect to return to a room full of devastation as the TACs would overturn beds, wall lockers, and of course the footlocker with all its contents not of only the offending candidate, but everyone else's also spilled on the floor. We watched and even laughed at the different things the TACs came up with to harass us, besides the constant pushups, to try and make you quit. For example, holding a military parade for a dead cockroach, including a coffin made from a match box with six pallbearers (I was one of them), marching to a slow drum roll around the Battalion area and then holding a solemn burial in a 6 by 6 foot grave with full military honors, taps and all. They had us conduct 50 yard dashes with filled sandbags in 90 degree plus temperatures until we could go no further due to the heat and humidity. Another was marching several miles at 22:00 hours in the remnants of a hurricane blowing in from the Gulf of Mexico, then trying to pitch shelter halves in winds reaching 40 miles an hour on Soldiers Field and sleeping the best we could in standing water for the remainder of the night. Last but not least allowing us to have a Pizza Party after being caught smuggling Pizzas into the building in trash cans. The problem was the party was held in the shower room under cold running water. Talk about a soggy mess. The TACs watched the party while eating one of the Pizzas at our expense. The 24 week course was difficult, but doable and in retrospect even funny when we went back and thought about it. Nonetheless we watched candidates dropped from the class either by failure to handle the harassment, the physical training or even the military education we were being taught to become effective leaders.

After reaching the 18th week of training we became senior candidates and things became better. The TACs eased up on some of the harassment even to the point of treating us with some respect for what we had accomplished and we now marched to all training rather than double timing. We also enjoyed a Company Ball, but were still not exempt from the spit shined floors, which we continued to do. In December 1964 some 150 students from class 10-64 were commissioned as new Infantry 2nd Lieutenants and were handed orders for their new assignments. Each of us were proud of our accomplishment and looked forward to our new assignments.

CHAPTER 2

AIRBORNE, RANGER, AND FORT ORD

Following Christmas leave, I along with approximately 30 of my classmates received orders to attend Airborne School (many of my classmates were prior service and were already airborne qualified). After the three week training accompanied by countless pushups handed out by the Airborne Cadre, we proudly received our Airborne Wings from Col Lamar Welch, the head of the Airborne Committee. I was then ordered to report to Ft Ord, California where i was assigned as a training officer to C Company, 4th Battalion, 1st Brigade, an Advanced Individual Training (AIT) Company. During the ensuing year I returned to Ft. Benning and attended the rigorous Army Ranger Training Course, considered one of the most difficult courses the Army conducts. The first Phase was three weeks at Fort Benning mainly devoted to physical conditioning, The Darby Queen - an arduous one mile long Obstacle Course containing some 20 obstacles that had to be negotiated over hilly terrain every day over the last two weeks of the Benning Phase, and learning basic patrolling techniques. Also included at the Benning Phase was instruction in hand-to-hand combat and bayonet training, mostly done in 90+ degree heat and the oppressive humidity of southern Georgia in July and August. The training in this phase culminated with a 12 mile timed road march in full combat gear with weapon. This was followed by the three week Mountain

Phase at Camp Frank Merrill near Dahlonega, Georgia. Mountain climbing techniques, rappelling, knot tying, stream crossings, and intensive patrolling made up most the training all with little or no sleep. Emphasis was on conducting reconnaissance patrols and raiding enemy fortifications in mountainous terrain at night. The third and last Phase was conducted at Camp Rudder located on Eglin Air Force Base in Florida. Also known as the Swamp Phase, training included stream crossings, small boat tactics and negotiating swamps in pursuit of enemy aggressors. The training culminated in a raid on an enemy base located on an island in the Gulf of Mexico and a picnic of alligator, raccoon, possum and various other exotic edibles prepared by the cadre at Camp Rudder. After nine grueling weeks of both intense physical and mental training with little or no sleep (on average 2-4 hours a night) I earned the much desired and sought after U.S. Army Ranger Tab and Diploma. Only 49% of those who started the course in July successfully completed it, one of the highest rates of graduation at that time.

I then returned to Fort Ord as the Executive/Training Officer in my previous Company. My commanding officer Captain John Gibbs, a West Point graduate, was so impressed that I had successfully completed Ranger Training he directed I lead all physical training requirements of the company. It actually turned out to be a blessing in disguise as I attained the best physical condition of my life, which would help tremendously in my upcoming assignment. Gibbs was from a family of West Pointers and all though likeable remained aloof from the cadre. I found all of the NCOs to be hard workers dedicated to the troops they led in training.

In January 1966 I faced a major decision, leave the US Army or contact my Branch Assignment Officer in Washington D.C. and volunteer to be placed on indefinite status, meaning as a reserve officer on active duty I would commit to stay on active duty as long as the Army needed me. I also affirmed I would be willing to volunteer to serve in Vietnam if I could be guaranteed an assignment to an airborne unit already in country, thinking either the 173rd Airborne Brigade or the 101st

Airborne Division. If he could not meet my request I would leave the Army in June 1966 after completing my commitment to the Army upon graduating from Infantry Officer Candidate School at Fort Benning. He agreed, asked me to forward my requests in writing thru my Chain of Command to the Infantry Assignments Branch in Washington, D.C. I complied that same day and within three weeks received word that my request for indefinite status had been approved and my orders for assignment to Vietnam was forthcoming. Several days later I received orders directing me to report to Travis AFB in California for further movement to the 90th Replacement Detachment, Republic of Vietnam. This was to be accomplished no later than early March 1966 following a 30 day leave. Although I had second thoughts about my decision there was no turning back and I began preparation for my move to the ancient and mysterious country of Vietnam.

I drove from Fort Ord, California, to my home in Virginia and said my farewells to family and friends. My closest friends and I managed to put away several cases of beer and several bottles of spirits during my all too short leave. On the day I left my Mother, who had held up bravely, was now teary eyed and held on to me like she would never let me go. This was not the first time she sent a soldier to war. My father served in the British Army from 1939 until 1945 during World War II as a corpsman, and my older brother served in the U.S Air Force in the late '50s/early '60s as a communications specialist. I eventually boarded a flight from Norfolk Naval Base, Virginia, on a Navy transport plane to Whidbey Island Naval Air Station near Seattle, Washington, then to the San Francisco/Oakland area in California.

On arrival, with time to kill, I sought out a nearby bar to have a beer before catching a bus to Travis AFB, California. I couldn't believe the reception I received when I entered the bar in uniform. Before I knew it I had several beers in front of me and a number of women in the bar had hugged and kissed me a several times over. The war in Vietnam was still popular at that time and I finally had to beg off and get to the Greyhound Station a short walk away to catch the bus to Travis. The trip to Travis took a little over an hour, enough time to sober up before reporting to the movement center where a hundred or so other military personnel were sitting around waiting for the flight to Vietnam, via Hickam AFB, Hawaii; Anderson AFB, Guam; and Clark Field in the Philippines. The flight in all would take about 24 hours so we were told, but the good news it would be by commercial jet liner. As usual with the military, after a lengthy wait we finally boarded and began our trip to the unknown, many of the troops on board knowing they would probably not survive their year in 'Nam.

CHAPTER 3

DEPARTURE, ARRIVAL, AND ASSIGNMENT

The large commercial PAN AM jet, after a lengthy flight, began a steep spiral into the Saigon International Airport at Tan Son Nhut, Republic of Vietnam. We had finally arrived after the roughly twenty four hour trek across what seemed the never ending blue Pacific. We had departed Travis AFB, California, on 16 March 1966 with stops in Honolulu, Hawaii, where we were told no one was to leave the airport waiting area (So much for seeing beautiful Hula dancers waiting to cover us with flowered Leis or handing us a great tasting Mai Tai). They did have coffee, tea or soft drinks available if we wanted them. About two hours later we were then on our way to Guam where the reception underwhelmed us. No beautiful scantily clad women nor senior officers and NCOs greeted us at roughly 0300 hours; just a couple of pissed of airmen who told us not to leave the terminal under any circumstances and to not sleep on the chairs/benches in the reception area. They did tell us coffee/sodas would be served at 0600 hours when the snack bar opened. This was greeted by cheers, until we found out we would be leaving at 0500. We were treated better at our next stop, Clark AFB in the Philippines. They let us stay in the terminal while the plane was refueled for the last leg of the trip to Vietnam. We were able to use the terminal restrooms to refresh ourselves, do our business, and then purchase coffee, donuts or other non-alcoholic refreshment from a small snack bar in the terminal. After a short wait we then boarded the aircraft and began the last leg of our journey to beautiful Saigon, the Paris of the Orient, where we would deplane to the sights, sounds, and the smells of the Orient which quickly overwhelmed our senses. The heat and humidity was oppressive and it felt like we were walking into a sauna, made even more so since I was wearing the Army Class A Green uniform per instructions in my orders.

Sergeants were screaming to follow them for check in and then movement to the 90th replacement detachment for in-country assignments while artillery was firing at some unseen enemy in the distance to the west/northwest of Saigon, fighter jets were taking of/ or landing and helicopters loaded with armaments were patrolling the perimeter to deter any ground attacks on the field. Airport vehicular traffic was moving quickly on the tarmac with seemingly no destination in mind, but somehow getting there, and crowds flowed toward the terminal building led by the ever present E-5s or SP-4s screaming out orders, "enlisted to the left, Officers to the Center, and NCOs to the right. You will be processed through here and before you know it will be on your way to your permanent units of assignment post haste. Charlie is waiting. " Coordinated bedlam at its best.

As we moved through the airport terminal I recognized one of my former OCS Tactical Officers, Captain Joseph Rodger, who was on his way back to the Land of the Big PX after having served a tour with Special Forces. He recognized me and asked where I was being assigned. I told him I was not sure, but it would be with an Airborne Unit, since I had requested this before volunteering for Vietnam and had been told the Army would honor my request. He wished me well, saying "you will need it" then added "keep your butt down, these guys are good." It was a lesson I took immediately to heart.

The cadre in charge finally moved us to a string of busses waiting near the terminal, loaded us and then moved on to the 90th Replacement for processing and room assignments prior to moving to our permanent units. I wondered why the buses had wire screens over the windows, then like a fool realized it was to prevent anyone trying to throw a hand grenade or other explosives through them. For all the confusion the process worked fairly well. We were assigned to buildings well bunkered by sandbags and told where the various facilities were located (i.e. Personnel, PX, Mess Halls, Clubs, etc.) in the compound. We were also informed assignments and movement to our new units would begin in the morning and for some it may take several days. We were also told the base was subject to rocket and mortar fire at times. Just what a newbie wanted to hear.

Since I had no appointments with personnel that day I went to the Officers Club for a beer and a hamburger. While there I met a Lieutenant, formerly of the 1st Infantry Division, who was processing out. I don't recall his name but he had been a platoon leader, had seen some heavy action and was glad it was over for him. He also passed on that the enemy I would be facing in the future were good, the second time that day I had been told this. After a couple of beers and aimless chatter, he suggested we hit downtown Saigon and have a few more beers, a steam bath and a massage. He said it might be the last one I would have for a while. This sounded good to me so of we went. We ended up drinking a couple of beers in a small hole in the wall bar with some scantily clad women and then headed for the steam bath and massage. I have to say the women were beautiful, with the exception of my masseuse who was a petite lady (probably in her mid-thirties but looked sixty), ugly as sin, and had only a few stained teeth. She led me to a shower where she bathed me then dried me off with a small towel. Next came a steam bath and the much needed massage. She placed me face down on a small table then proceeded to beat the living hell out of me. The piece de la resistance, however, was when she climbed on the table and proceeded to walk and dance on my back. This petite little lady now felt like she weighed 300 pounds and I thought my spine was going to be pushed through my stomach. To this day I believe she was a Viet Cong supporter and it was her way of welcoming me to the "Nam". After this experience I was more than ready to get back to my billet and bed. I was not impressed by my first and only night in the capitol city and was looking forward to some much needed sleep; however, no one mentioned the units around Saigon would be firing H&I fires (harassment and interdiction fire) and that aircraft and helicopters would be flying in and out of the airfield all night. So much for a good night's rest.

CHAPTER 4

IN COUNTRY ASSIGNMENT

The next morning after breakfast I was told to report to in-processing. When I arrived I was motioned to a desk where a SP4 clerk was waiting. He greeted me with a friendly smile and said "Sir, congratulations you are going to the II Corps Tactical Zone for assignment with the 1st Air Cavalry Division." I immediately interjected "there must be a mistake. My Branch Assignment Officer in D.C. assured me, since I volunteered for Vietnam, I would be assigned to an Airborne Unit." I could not understand why all of a sudden I was now being assigned to the 1st Cavalry and not the 101st Airborne Division or the 173rd Airborne Brigade. He just smiled and said "maybe they can straighten it out once you get there, but until then there is nothing I can do. Your flight to An Khe is leaving tomorrow morning so have your bags packed and be on the plane for the flight up country." Needless to say I was totally pissed. In my mind the frigging Army had screwed me and not given me the airborne assignment I had requested. I asked to speak to a senior officer. The Specialist left and came back with a Major who glared at me and simply stated, "Lieutenant you have your orders. Be on that flight to An Khe. If you have a beef take it up when you sign in with the Cav." End of discussion. Saluting smartly I went to pack my duffle for the flight as ordered, seething and wondering where the hell is An Khe.

The flight north the next morning was by Air Force C-130 from Tan Son Nhut to an old French Airfield on the outskirts of the small village of An Tuc, also known as An Khe, with several stops in-between to drop of supplies and personnel returning to their units. During the flight I overheard several Captains talking. All expressed the hope they would be assigned to the 1st Brigade of the Cav rather than the 2nd or 3rd Brigades. To me it seemed kind of strange and I finally asked one "why the 1st Brigade." His response, "The 1st is the Airborne Brigade, the others are all straight leg outfits." I was immediately elated now knowing my assignment officer had upheld his end of the bargain, even though I still had some trepidation, knowing the Cav could still assign me wherever they needed officers.

We arrived at a former French airfield, which was located in a large valley surrounded by median size hills to tall mountains, one to the west displaying a huge 1st Cavalry Patch. I later found out the mountain was known as Hon Kong and it overlooked the base camp, known as Camp Radcliff. The camp was named after Major Donald Radcliff, the first service member killed in the 1st Cavalry Division after its arrival. A signal detachment was located on its summit. Raucous monkeys kept them company.

We unloaded our gear from the aircraft before it taxied and took of leaving the group of us wondering where the hell we were since no one was there to meet us. Eventually several vehicles did appeared and we and our gear were transported through the village of An Khe to Camp Radcliff, Base Camp of the 1st Cavalry Division. It had been hacked out of the jungle to the north of An Khe and contained the world's largest helipad which was known as the Golf Course. We were dropped at the Division Personnel Center where we were given our final assignments. The three Captains and several Lieutenants who were on the flight with me wound up assigned to the 3rd Brigade, also known as the Gary Owen Brigade, much to their great displeasure. I, on the other hand was assigned to the 1st Battalion, 8th Cavalry Regiment (Airborne), the only officer sent to the Airborne Brigade. Needless to say I was elated even though I still did not know what my ultimate assignment would be on arrival at the 1/8th. Shortly thereafter a jeep arrived and I was driven to my new Battalion area, a conglomeration of tents and semi-permanent wooden buildings, but mostly tents.

CHAPTER 5

INTRODUCTION AND ASSIGNMENT TO THE 1/8TH

On arrival I reported to the S-1 (Personnel) Section and signed in as the newest member of the "Jumping Mustangs", the nickname associated with the Battalion since the unit crest depicted a jumping horse. I was introduced to several NCOs and enlisted men, including Sergeant Major Herbert McCullah. I also met Lt Robert Weary, the Assistant S-1, who greeted me warmly and then escorted me to the Medical Platoon tent where I would stow my gear and spend the night until the Battalion Commander made the final decision where I would assume my duties. Not long after Lt Weary returned and escorted me to Headquarters to meet the Battalion Commander, LtCol Levin Broughton, a West Point graduate, who had only earlier that day taken command from LtCol Kenneth Mertel. Mertel had commanded the battalion since its formation at Fort Benning in 1965, had been promoted to Colonel and was being assigned as the Assistant Brigade Commander.

Fig 1. LtCol Levin Broughton *Fig 2. LtCol Kenneth Mertel*

Col Broughton greeted me with a smile and warm welcome to the Battalion. After pleasantries he told me he was assigning me to Bravo Company as a platoon leader. The company was commanded by Captain Roy D. Martin. Martin, he explained, was a veteran of the Korean War and a former member, Executive Officer, and Commander of the vaunted U.S. Army Golden Knights Parachute Team and he considered Martin the best company commander in the Battalion, by far. This was based on the assessments he had received from Mertel when he briefed Broughton before the change of command.

Fig 3 CPT Roy Martin, C.O., Bravo Company, 1/8th Cavalry (ABN)

He added that I would stay at Headquarters that night and would join Bravo Company in the morning. I returned to the Medical Platoon tent to spend the evening and to try to get some rest which proved difficult since all night long an artillery unit (later found out the 2/19 Artillery Battalion) located adjacent to the Battalion area fired Harassment and Interdiction (H&I) fires while Huey helicopter gunships patrolled the perimeter throughout the night to preclude any attempts at attacking the base at night.

CHAPTER 6

INTRODUCTION TO B COMPANY 1/8TH CAVALRY (ABN)

The next day, March 21st, 1966 I reported to the Bravo Company orderly room and was greeted by 1st Sergeant Ray Poynter, from Berryville, Arkansas a grizzled veteran of WWII and Korea. He was the epitome in my mind of the perfect 1st SGT.

Fig 4. 1st SGT Ray Poynter

He, in turn, introduced me to Lt Michael Livengood, the 2/19th artillery forward observer assigned to the company; Sergeant Enoch Copeland, the Operations NCO; and several others at Company Headquarters. He next introduced me to 1st Lieutenant John Langston, the Company Executive Officer (XO), who made it abundantly clear that he was the senior Lieutenant in the company and that I would address him as such whenever I talked to him as he chewed on an ever present cigar. I thought to myself, what an arrogant prick, and took an immediate dislike towards him. I thought to myself I hope to hell the other Lieutenants in the Company were not of this persuasion. Luckily this proved to be correct when I met the other officers. Everyone else at the Company Headquarters greeted me warmly and made me feel at home.

Captain Martin was unavailable when I arrived so 1SGT Poynter escorted me to the Platoon Leaders tent to stow my gear and to introduce the other Lieutenants in the Company; 2nd Lt William (Bill) Hughes from Cordele, Georgia, Platoon Leader of the 3rd Platoon and 1st Lt Jared (Jerry) East, from Lake Charles, Louisiana, Platoon Leader of the 4th Platoon.

Fig 5. 2nd Lt Bill Hughes   *Fig 6 2nd LT Robert Crum*

2nd Lt Robert (Bob) Crum from Houston, Texas, Platoon Leader of the 1st Platoon was on a patrol with his platoon and would return later in the afternoon. Bob was the newest of the Lieutenants, having joined the Company about a month prior to my arrival while Hughes and East were veterans having trained at Fort Benning then shipped on the USN Ship Geiger to Vietnam with the 1st Cavalry Division when it deployed. Hughes and Crum, like I, were Infantry OCS graduates while East graduated from the ROTC program at Louisiana Tech. I found these leaders to be affable, capable and willing to assist me in any way to adjust to my new situation. In direct contrast to Langston, they were all were warm and willing to go out of their way to assist me to adjust. Our living quarters left much to be desired, a small hexagonal tent with just enough room for four people and their gear. For what it was worth this was to be my new home whenever we were in Base Camp at Anh Khe which in retrospect turned out to be seldom.

Captain Martin soon returned to the Company Headquarters and I was summoned to meet with him. Martin a veteran of the Korean War, was from Laurel, Mississippi, had short reddish hair, was a no nonsense type individual, but was warm with a dry sense of humor. Although in awe of his previous army history I took an immediate liking to him and felt comfortable around him. He welcomed me to the unit and said he was assigning me to the second platoon as a replacement for 1st Lt Jack Peevy, who had been seriously wounded and evacuated back to the United States (I later found out Peevy had been shot seven times. He not only survived, but remained on active duty eventually retiring as a Colonel).

Fig 7 1Lt Jack Peevy

The Captain stated I would spend the first week under the tutelage of Lt Hughes and his platoon so I could learn how the company operated in the field and to help acclimate me to the heat and humidity. This was fine with me since I was a little leery, in fact scared shitless, of my ability to lead a platoon of men in combat. All of the lieutenants assured me I would do just fine. Martin also went on to say the NCOs of the company were the best in the Battalion, especially Sergeant First Class James Johnson, the Platoon Sergeant of the 2nd Platoon who had been serving as the Platoon Leader since Peevy had been wounded.

Fig 8. PSG James Johnson

Martin indicated the conversation was over but asked me to meet him at the Battalion Officers Club after dinner so we could continue our conversation. I returned to the platoon leader's tent, wondering if Johnson would resent me replacing him as the Platoon Leader.

Bob Crum and his platoon had returned and I was introduced to him. I liked him immediately. Around 1830 hours the other Lieutenants and I headed to the club, me to meet with Martin, and the others to play cards or have a few drinks. Martin was sitting at the bar having a Coke when we arrived. Hughes and East headed for the poker table where a game was already in progress and I sat down next to Captain Martin.

He asked what I would like to drink and I said a beer would be fine. After some casual conversation, like where I was born, where I was from in the States, where I went to college, and how long had I been in the Army he asked if I had ever hunted while growing up and if I was any good at it. I thought this was kind of a strange question and answered, "Yes Sir, I grew up hunting rabbit, squirrel, and deer since I was 12 years old and managed to put meat on the table from time to time." He smiled kind of wryly and said, "When we go out on operations against the Viet Cong and the PAVN (People's Army of Vietnam) if you apply the same sneak and peek principles you did when you were hunting, you will do okay." He added, "Take care of your men at all times and listen to your NCOs. You have some of the best there are, again praising Platoon Sergeant Johnson as a great Airborne NCO who has excelled in leading the platoon, again bringing me some trepidation as to my ability to lead a platoon of men in combat.

Following our conversation he then proceeded to introduce to me to Captain Russell Ramsey, HQs Company; Charles Stone, A Company; Captain William (Bill) Mozey, C Company; and several other officers at the bar, including Major Propes, Battalion S3 and Major Hermann, the Battalion XO. All appeared capable leaders in attitude and bearing. Martin mentioned the Battalion was actually on a stand down because of the Change of Command ceremony that had been held the day before and that was why so many officers were in the club that evening. He assured me that in several days the units of the battalion would again be moving out to the field on operations. Martin then excused himself and returned to the Company area, while I had a couple more beers and met and chatted with a number of Lieutenants from other companies including Roger Talmadge, former Executive Officer (XO) of B Company and now serving as the Battalion S-2;

Fig 9. Roger Talmadge, Former Executive Officer of B Company

Dennis Aschenbrenner, Ed Doubet, Bill Onstott, Warren Boyette, John Pape, Pat Grenier, Jerry Houchens, Jim Stotts, Frank Vavrek, Jimmie Nickels, Frank Spiers, Jon Williams, Waymon Elrod, Albert Hayes, Al Salazar, and a few more from the other companies in the Battalion. Most of them I would never see again during my year in Vietnam and some; Aschenbrenner, Hayes, Pape, Spiers and Elrod would later become casualties of the war.

Hughes, East and I headed back to the Company around 2200 hours to retire for the night. Crum had left earlier to write home to his wife. About the time we prepared to bed down a huge rat about the size of a house cat tried to occupy the same space as Bill Hughes, jumping on his chest as he reclined on his cot. All hell broke loose as Bill vacated the bed tearing down his mosquito net and a bunch of his gear and running for the opening. Jerry was attempting to chase the rat with his entrenching tool, but was unsuccessful as it scurried out through the door. Crum, who had been sitting on his bed penning a letter to his wife, was now standing on his cot, writing paper and pen on the floor, and I was glued to the floor petrified that rats were so big in Vietnam.

I swear they looked as big as alley cats. The chaos soon returned to normal and we all bedded down for the night. Shortly thereafter I could hear what sounded like the patter of little feet on the top of the tent and then a swishing motion. I rolled over and asked "what the hell is that." The response from East was the rats were playing on top of the tent and to just disregard them. Yeah, easier said than done, after hearing that I was awake most of the night.

Over the next several day's familiarization of the Company and Battalion area as well as personnel continued. A single dirt road ran through the battalion area with Headquarters near the top of the road facing the golf course, along with the mess hall, officers club, NCO Club and Enlisted Club all near the entrance to the battalion area. The company areas were aligned along the road in a general North to South direction on the east side of the dirt road. Supply and various HQ elements were to the west of the road as I recall. The Battalion Helipad, known as the Mustang Pad, was situated to the south end of the Battalion and across another road from Bravo Company's area. Along this road was the 2/19th Artillery Battalion, the Division Military Intelligence Company and the 8th Combat Engineer Battalion. The opposite direction on this road lead to the shower facility and the Song Ba, a river, which skirted the Division Base Camp to the East and North.

I was introduced to each of the senior NCOs; SFC James Johnson, 2nd Platoon; SSG Bobby James, 3rd Platoon; SSG Winfred Bledsoe, 4th Platoon; and SFC William Robinson, 1st Platoon. With the exception of SSG Bledsoe all were seasoned veterans having deployed with the Division in September 1965. Most had also served in the Korean War as well. Bledsoe had been in country since December 1965, but had become a hardened veteran in the short time he was there. Loud and profane his men loved him. I was also introduced to the NCOs of the 2nd Platoon, SSgt Paul Hemphill and SGTs Arsenio Lujan, Antonio Lopez, Leroy Christian, and Gerald Hoover and then met the men of the platoon. I was impressed with all of them and their dedication, sense of duty, and professionalism. They appeared to be a strong fighting force and well trained. I would soon discover I was not wrong in my evaluation of these men. I am sure each of them were also measuring me as their new commander and wondering what the future would bring under my leadership.

CHAPTER 7

OPERATION LINCOLN

On 24 March 1966 we received an alert order from Captain Martin to begin preparation for movement on the morning of the 25th to an area to the far west of An Khe in the high plateau of Pleiku Province. The operation was named Lincoln and it would involve the entire 1st Brigade and its supporting units. The 1/8th would be the lead Battalion, and Bravo Company would be the first unit into the Landing Zone located just to the northeast of the Chu Pong Mastiff, an area well known for the Battle of LZ X-Ray in November 1965. The remainder of the Battalion would follow us into the LZ, named Bear, with the mission to search and destroy any North Vietnamese and Viet Cong forces in the area. It was to be the largest air assault in the young history of the 1st Cav Division in Vietnam; moving an entire Battalion in one lift. We would be followed by the remainder of the 1st Brigade. On receiving the order the Lieutenants and Sergeants began preparing themselves and their men for the coming operation.

At approximately 0600 hours on the 25th, while in the final phases of preparing to mount up with their gear a tragic accident occurred. One of the men, SP4 Charles Harmon, accidently mishandled a grenade that was attached to his web gear hanging from a tent pole in the squad tent, causing an explosion that killed himself and wounded eight others in the squad who were also in their final preparation before moving out. All the men were from the 2nd Platoon, the platoon I was slated to command. Not a great way to be introduced to the horrors of war and the responsibilities of command. The Platoon Sergeant, Squad Leaders, and medics quickly took charge and evacuated the wounded to the Battalion Aid Station where they were quickly triaged and then moved to the 15th Medical Battalion Hospital close to the Division Headquarters area. Surprisingly most of the men wounded would later return to duty with the Company. Even with this horrific accident, the remainder of the Company continued to prepare for the move.

Martin called the Company together and conducted a final briefing before we boarded the lift ships for movement to the Area of Operations near the Cambodian border. He said he would be in the lead along with Hughes' Platoon. He and his Radio Operators would be on the 2nd Huey, and Lt Hughes, myself and others from his platoon would make up the remainder of the lead element into Landing Zone Bear. The LZ was about 10 kilometers southeast of the Duc Co Special Forces Camp, near the Cambodian border, and just to the north of the Ia Drang river valley and the Chu Pong Mastiff, the scene of heavy fighting in October and November 1965 by elements of the 1st Cavalry Division, including the 1/8th, and a North Vietnamese Division. (Note: During that operation Alpha Company, led by CPT Theodore Danielson, from the 1/8th made the first night air assault of the war into an LZ surrounded by NVA soldiers. Elsewhere Charlie Company, after a fierce fight, captured a NVA Field Hospital).

The 1st Platoon, led by Lt Crum, would come in behind us, followed by the 2nd and then the 4th Platoon. As we secured our portion at the Landing Zone the remainder of the battalion would land and take up their assigned positions on the perimeter until the entire unit was on the ground. The Battalion Headquarters would come in last. A second lift containing a battery from the 2/19th Artillery would follow providing the needed direct artillery fire to the battalion as necessary. Martin then led us in prayer, wished us success, and moved the company to the Mustang Pad to mount our helicopters for the assault. Spirits were high as we were finally going into action rather than the mundane day to day duty that was being performed while in base camp.

Around 0900 hours our helicopter support began arriving for pickup at the Mustang Pad. The liftoff went without a hitch and the Company followed by other elements of the Battalion were soon winging west at 3000 feet toward the Pleiku Plateau generally following Highway 19, which ran from Qui Nhon on the coast of the South China Sea to the Cambodian border in the West. The doors on our chopper were open and unlike on the ground it was cool, almost to the point of being cold. We soon flew over the Mang Yang Pass, which Bill Hughes explained was the location where French Mobile Group 100 was ambushed and decimated by a large Viet Minh Force during the First Indochina War. It was one of the most devastating defeats in French Army history. Of some 3,500 troops making up Mobile Group 100 approximately 500 were killed, 600 wounded, and 800 captured during the battle and coupled with the defeat of the French at Dien Bien Phu led to the withdrawal of the French from Indo-China.

Once through the pass the vast Pleiku Plateau came into view. The scenery was beautiful with rice paddies merging with heavily wooded jungle and mountains in the distance towards the Cambodian/Laotian borders. You could feel a shift in the body language of the troops on board our Huey. They had been here before during the Ia Drang Campaign in October and November 1965 and were leery of what would befall us as we began our approach to the LZ. I was about to make my first combat air assault and did not know what to expect. The order was given by Hughes to the others on board our helicopter to "lock and load."

As I looked to the west I could see what appeared to be a large opening in the distance and I deduced this was the Landing Zone we had been briefed on. The Lift Ships began their descent toward the ground and as I watched I started seeing explosions on the ground. Our gunship escorts began firing rockets and machine guns on the edge of the opening and almost immediately the machine gunner on the right side of our Huey began firing. To be blunt I was scared shitless and began searching frantically for enemy soldiers on the ground to fire at, but could not discern any movement or firing from the ground at all. I kept asking myself what the hell are they shooting at and thought the enemy must be really well concealed. Before I knew it the ships set down and the troops immediately headed for the tree line, firing in a controlled manner as they went. Martin and Hughes were bellowing out orders. As they neared the tree line the troops under the supervision of their squad leaders dropped to the ground and took up firing positions. It was then I finally realized we were not receiving and had never received any incoming fire. I turned to Hughes and asked what the firing was all about. He smiled wryly and said, "Standard Operating Procedure when we assault into a new Landing Zone. We don't want to be surprised should the VC/NVA have been waiting for us, it helps keep their heads down, allowing us to land." He ginned sheepishly and said "guess we should have told you that." To me confusion seemed to reign supreme as the squad leaders, Platoon Sergeants and Platoon leaders moved people into defensive positions, but it in fact was well practiced movements to allow the remainder of the Battalion to close on the LZ. Several small squad sized patrols were sent out to recon the immediate area around the LZ, but no enemy forces were encountered.

By early that evening the LZ had been firmly established, defensive positions dug and hot chow was being prepared. Night settled in fairly quickly and instructions were passed on for manning the defensive perimeter for the night. With the exception of a man dropping a mortar round down the barrel of a mortar tube the wrong way and the resulting "oh shit" before the crew under the close supervision of their squad leader successfully removed the round to the great relief of everyone in the vicinity all else was quiet. The remainder of the night passed peacefully, except for the occasional boom of artillery or mortars as they fired Harassment and Interdiction fires (H&I fires) at preplanned positions. This was to keep enemy soldiers or units from moving toward the Landing Zone along the most obvious routes of approach.

Early the next morning Martin gave orders for the platoons to begin aggressive patrolling around the LZ in a cloverleaf pattern. I was to accompany the Third Platoon which was to conduct a search to the east and south of the LZ to locate any enemy forces in the area and engage them. It had been reasonably mild, temperature wise, when we started, but as the day wore on the heat became damn near unbearable, at least in my mind. Hughes and his platoon members; however, did not appeared fazed in the least. I recall us moving up the side of a fairly large hill to the south of the LZ, which I believe was probably part of the Chu Pong Mastiff, then sweeping back to rejoin the company at the LZ. The patrol was insignificant and uneventful inasmuch as we made no contact nor did we see any signs or enemy or civilian activity during the patrol. Hughes did point our several termite hills and explained the VC/NVA dug into them and prepared firing positions that were almost impossible to destroy. It was all a learning process for me as I watched the men of the platoon move in a diamond formation which would allow them to immediately assume a defensive perimeter should contact be made. As a platoon leader I knew I would use this same formation whenever the terrain allowed me to do so. None of the other platoon patrols searching their sectors made contact or saw anyone either. This turned out to be the norm for the remaining time we spent on the operation, search daily in the blistering heat, with no results.

After the patrol with the 3rd Platoon, I met that evening with Platoon Sergeant Johnson and the Squad Leaders of the 2nd Platoon, a kind of a meet and greet session, now that we were in the field. I was stunned when one of the squad leaders, Sergeant Gerald Hoover, out of the blue made it clear he did not want to serve as he put it "with a fucking new guy", namely me even though he had not been on a single operation or patrol which I participated in. Taken by surprise and, although being totally upset with his request, I told him I would see what could be worked out. Later that evening, after talking with Bill Hughes and PSG Johnson, I found Hughes had a squad leader he was having problems with and we agreed to swap Hoover for Sergeant Dewey Underwood. Captain Martin and 1st SGT Poynter were notified of our plan and neither voiced a problem as long as all parties were in agreement with the switch. Hoover and Underwood agreed and the switch was made. Hoover went to the 3st Platoon and Underwood became one of my squad leaders in the 2nd platoon. Martin, during the meeting, informed me he was completely happy with my progress and Bill Hughes' report and therefore I was to take command of the 2nd Platoon immediately.

The remainder of the operation was primarily platoon and company size patrols. On one of the company patrols we were accompanied by a newsman (If I correctly recall I believe John Laurence) and a cameraman both from CBS news. Within 30 minutes they began complaining of the heat and pleaded for Captain Martin to call a helicopter to fly them back to the LZ. That was a no go for Martin who told them to gut it out, we would return to the LZ in a few hours if we did not make contact. About 45 minutes later we came upon a small stream and as we crossed a huge lizard, probably 5-6 foot long, burst from the bank and splashed across the stream. Needless to say it scared the crap out of us and chaos broke out as troops scrambled every which way to get out of its path. Luckily no one fired and it soon escaped into to the safety of the surrounding underbrush.

Shortly thereafter Martin called for a break. As one trooper leaned back against a tree he was stung in the shoulder/neck area by a large scorpion, about the size of a hand. The sting was severe and he began to experience swelling in the neck area. He also began having breathing problems and the medics treated him for anaphylactic shock. A medevac helicopter was called to evacuate him to the aid station at LZ Bear for treatment.

When it arrived the CBS reporter and cameraman received their wish and wasted no time jumping on the helicopter and riding back to the rear with the ailing soldier. Again, our cross country jaunt was just that. We neither saw nor heard any movement by enemy forces as we moved back to LZ Bear.

During the remainder of Operation Lincoln I commanded the 2nd Platoon and we continued to patrol aggressively within the assigned

Area of Operations (AO), which was adjacent to the Cambodian border. Although we and other elements of the Battalion and Brigade received sporadic sniper fire from across the border we were not allowed to fire back and never made contact with any significant enemy force. No one from Bravo Company was injured by any of these minor enemy harassment firings and I was well pleased with the performance of the platoon. I realized they were professionals by any stretch of the imagination, well trained and in excellent physical condition.

Operation Lincoln; however, turned out to be a dry hole for the most part and after a week of operations the company moved back to an area called the Oasis, a Landing Zone southwest of Pleiku, for resupply and preparation to move back to Camp Radcliff. I had finally become acclimated to the high temperatures and humidity. While at this location Bravo Company was assigned the task of securing a portion of the perimeter. Part of our security force was a platoon size element of supply personnel, cooks, and assorted rear area element personnel. Martin, in what I believe was an intentional plan, assigned these men to me as well as the designated area we were to secure. It became one of the longest nights of my life. To our front approximately 300-400 yards was a Montagnard village and no sooner had the sun gone down when they began chanting and beating on drums, logs and whatever in some sort of celebration. One of the men on the perimeter immediately fired his weapon, believing we were under some sort of assault. Of course Martin contacted me immediately and asked about the firing. I was already headed toward the foxhole and had found out the man was, like me, new and inexperienced and believed an attack on his position was about to take place. I assured him that I did not believe this to be the case, notified the Captain and headed back to my Command Post. No sooner had I arrived at this position when another burst of gunfire from my sector of the perimeter rang out and Martin again asked what the hell was going on. I again moved around the perimeter and found another young soldier who claimed he heard movement to his front. I pointed out there was a village out in front of him and was sure that was what he was hearing. I made my way back and reported again that all was okay, I just had a lot of inexperienced and scared men manning the line, including myself. He responded "get them under control", just as another burst of fire went off. Now I was getting pissed. Again, making my way to the perimeter, hoping like all hell I didn't miscalculate and end up being in front of friendly positions, I found the culprit and asked "what the hell are you shooting at." the same response, "I heard movement." For the third time I explained there was a village to our front some 3 to 4 hundred yards away and that the sounds he was hearing were in all likelihood coming from the hamlet. He agreed and I started back to my position. I didn't make it 30 yards before another defensive position fired. This time I was totally pissed. I scrambled back and went to every position and told each "if I hear one more burst of gunfire you better be ready to show me a dead Victor Charlie. Do I make myself abundantly clear?" Thank God the remainder of what was left of the night stayed calm, although I did not get any sleep as I lay waiting for the next burst of fire. The following day I reported back to the Company CP and Captain Martin, with a small grin on his face, asked how the night went. I just shrugged and said "As best it could with what I had to work with." His response was "you did a good job" and with that I went back to my platoon to get them ready for movement as the company was returning to An Khe base camp that afternoon.

We had spent a little over a week on Operation Lincoln. No large enemy forces had been encountered by most of Cavalry units taking part in the operation, except for the 1/12th Cav and the 1/9th Scouts. The scouts had located a number of NVA/VC just to the south of the Chu Pong Massif in elephant grass and had engaged. The force turned out to be more than they could handle and a company from the 1/12th was brought in to reinforce them. They ended up in a major battle with an estimated force of 100 NVA regulars requiring even more reinforcements, including air and artillery to be brought in. When the battle ended the two US units had suffered moderate casualties while the NVA, suffered heavy casualties and fled back to the safety of their sanctuaries in Cambodia.

CHAPTER 8

BASE CAMP AND HIGHWAY 19 SECURITY

The first mission for the Battalion on returning from Operation Lincoln was Base Camp security on the Green Line and highway duty securing Highway 19 from An Khe to the Mang Yang Pass west of Camp Radcliff. Since this was near the area French Mobile Group had suffered a monumental defeat at the hands of the Viet Minh in 1954 it left me with sobering thoughts as we began our highway duty.

Our assigned mission was to protect the bridges and convoys as they moved fuel and supplies from Qui Nhon on the coast to the cities of Pleiku and Kontum in the west. Almost every bridge had been blown and bypasses erected around them by the engineers allowed convoys and civilian traffic to move freely along the highway. Our job was to make sure the road and bypasses remained intact. We accomplished this with no contact with enemy forces, but the duty was not without incident. Shortly after assuming the highway duty I was called to the Command Group and was informed by Captain Martin that I was to lead a squad size patrol plus medical personnel to a Montagnard village to assist in a MEDCAP (Medical Civic Actions Program) mission. He said there could be a problem when we arrived since the village had mistakenly been hit by friendly artillery fire and we should be prepared for a hostile reception. Damn, just what I needed, but being the new guy on the block I accepted the mission without further discussion, since I also knew it would be useless.

Soon the Medical Team, a Doctor, several medics, and a USAID representative, a Vietnamese Major and an interpreter arrived and we set out. We traveled several miles west towards Pleiku and then turned to the North on a dirt trail leading into heavy jungle. Several miles later with the pucker factor up we arrived at a sizeable opening containing a small village with long bamboo structures on stilts about six feet of the ground. Several had been damaged, but not significantly. No inhabitants were visible, but we noticed several small cooking fires smoldering around the area indicating a human presence nearby. The Vietnamese officer and interpreter began calling out and minutes later a few small muscular armed male villagers appeared from the surrounding jungle carrying crossbows, large machete/knives, or spears and angry expressions on their faces. A heated discussion followed. I had the interpreter explain we were there to offer apologies for the damage the artillery caused and to provide assistance, including medical help for any villagers needing it. This seemed to placate the men somewhat and one signaled back to the jungle and about 100 more Montganards; men, women, and children, emerged from the surrounding jungle. The men encircled our small team, the women and children hung back, with the smaller children shyly hanging on to the back of their mother's skirts while peeking around at us. Most of the women were bare breasted and for the most part all were chewing on what I later learned was betel nuts which left their teeth red stained. More discussions ensued and soon the medical team was allowed to set up and begin treating both injured and sick villagers. The remainder of our team began passing out clothing, food, tools and small trinkets around the village. Tensions quickly eased and about two hour later we left the village after partaking in some food and drinks offered by the villagers. I have no idea what the meal consisted of but suspected monkey or perhaps water buffalo.

This was my first encounter with these people of the mountains and I found once the MEDCAP began their work the people became extremely warm, friendly, and gracious. I did detect; however, the same was not shown by the Vietnamese Officer or the interpreter. They both showed a certain amount of superiority, contempt and indifference to the villagers. It was also obvious the feeling was mutually held by the Montagnards. I later found this same attitude was held by most Vietnamese towards these people of the mountains. Our mission done we left the village with a sense of accomplishment and returned to Company control while the Medical Team returned to An Khe. The highway duty lasted about week and then we returned to base camp where we resumed patrolling around the base camp.

A week later the company was ordered to conduct an air assault into the mountains about ten miles south of An Khe on a one-day search mission. The pickup took place from the Mustang Pad located just south of the Battalion area. Third Platoon would lead the assault, followed by my platoon, then the First. As the Company began boarding it became evident there was a problem. The lift ships which were designed originally to carry two pilots, two crew members and 11 passengers, were usually limited to 6-8 fully equipped troops in the Central Highlands of Vietnam because of difficulty obtaining lift due of the extremely high temperatures, high humidity, and altitude in the mountains. As with all well planned operations a SNAFU (Situation Normal all F****d Up) had reared its ugly head. The plan called for eight men to a chopper with the crew, but it was now obvious this was not going to work. Troops began unloading one at a time as the pilots kept attempting to lift off. Finally it was determined that the ships could only accommodate a total of eight men per ship. To allow for more troops on the ground the decision was made to leave the door gunner at the Battalion LZ and add one additional infantryman who would man the machine gun position. Since six ships were assigned for each lift it meant the first lift would handle the Command Group and about half of the third platoon, about 30 men in all instead of the 48 troops the lift normally could handle. The operation finally got underway and headed for the designated LZ with a flight and turnaround time of about twenty minutes. We soon learned the 1st Platoon was on the ground but was receiving sporadic

And the Tears Flowed

fire and to prepare to arrive under fire also, although the troops on the ground should be able to suppress any hostile action as we assaulted in.

The remainder of the 1st platoon and half of my platoon arrived about 30 minutes later, but no fire was directed at us. I moved quickly to the Command Group location after deploying my troops to find out what was going on and what he wanted me to do with my platoon. Martin said that on their arrival they received light small arms fire and, believe it or not, arrows fired from crossbows. Lt Bill Hughes had been shot through the calf with one of these arrows and was being evacuated on the helicopters heading back for the next lift. The wound, although it did not look that serious, caused some concern because of the possibility of poison and infection. Hughes was placed on a helicopter and evacuated back to Camp Radcliff.

The C.O. then said as soon as the remainder of my platoon arrived he wanted us to move to the west/northwest and follow a heavy traveled trail up the side a mountain and search for possible enemy or enemy base camps. He said the 3rd Platoon, when they closed on the LZ, would sweep to the area south/south east of the Landing Zone and conduct a search of that area. The 1st Platoon would remain where they were, secure the LZ and reinforce either of the platoons should contact be made.

Once the remainder of my platoon were on the ground we began our movement to search the area designated by Captain Martin. The progress was slow as we began our ascent up the mountain. Because of the dense undergrowth and tall trees we were basically bound to the fairly wide and well used trail going up the mountain. We did not know what to expect, but we knew we didn't like being confined to a trail. SGT Antonio Lopez's squad led the way with PVT Ned Beazley on point. Interestingly I had helped put Beazley through Advance Training at Ft Ord in late Fall, 1965. Progress was slow and about half way up by my estimation and frequent progress reports, Beazley suddenly stopped and held his hand up as a signal for the rest of us to do the same. He turned to tell Lopez he had spotted a booby trap on the trail above him. As he turned to point out the trap he inadvertently hit the trip wire and was shot through the right shoulder by six foot long spear. It penetrated completely through the shoulder and the point was protruding out his back; however, had he not turned it would have certainly pierced his chest and in all likelihood it would have been fatal. He was bleeding profusely and in severe pain. The Platoon Medic, Sp4 Adell Alston, began working on him immediately and was able to stop the major bleeding and stabilize him. He did not remove the spear for fear he would do more damage, but with the help of others did remove most of the shaft.

Fig 10. SP4 Adell Alston

The immediate problem was we were in a location where we could not call in a Medevac helicopter to extract Beazley. We would have to return to the valley below, before reaching our objective, the top of the mountain. I contacted the Command Group and relayed we were returning to the valley floor and asked them to call for a Medevac once we neared the valley floor and have them contact me for coordinates for extraction. They acknowledged they would comply. I could still hear sporadic fire from the valley below and indicating some enemy activity was still ongoing. I had the medic prepare Beazley for movement back down the mountain. Once he finished we began moving back towards the valley floor. It was even slower going down as we had to stop and change the two helpers every 50 meters or so since Beazley was a large man. Also, even though he had been administered morphine, he was still in pain.

As we neared the valley floor we came under sporadic, but inaccurate fire by snipers. The Medevac which had arrived on the scene contacted me and said they were inbound and asked what the enemy situation was. Knowing if I reported we were receiving fire he would not land I told him I was receiving steady static over the radio and I was having trouble hearing him. I passed on the coordinates of an LZ where he could land. He repeated several times he needed to know the situation on the ground and I continued to say I could not understand, because of static. Finally, he turned on approach and landed. We loaded Beazley on board while the pilot gave me hell saying he received fire on his approach to the landing area. I just shrugged my shoulders as we got Beazley on board and on his way to treatment. The wound turned out to be his ticket home as he was evacuated all the way back to the States.

Since we were now in the valley, Martin ordered both platoons back to the LZ for extraction back to Camp Radcliffe. As I recall several other troops were slightly wounded by booby traps and punji stakes, but no firm contact with the enemy could be established. The Battalion Commander agreed and ordered our extraction.

After a couple of days in the Company area we assumed duty on the Green Line, the defensive perimeter that surrounded Camp Radcliffe. Little did I know that the Engineers who had supervised the construction of the Green Line had laid in lanes of fire for machine guns occupying the perimeter that we were supposed to use. I made my own recon of the perimeter and not liking what I saw, changed the machine gun positions. To this day I don't know if anyone realized I had done this. The worse part of Green Line duty for me was having to walk the line at night checking the defensive positions. Even though built to support three men per position (meaning two could sleep, while one pulled two hours on watch, then they would rotate) I invariably found everyone on the position asleep, including squad leaders. Hell I knew I couldn't give them all Article 15s (non-judicial punishment for minor offenses that does not warrant trial by court martial) so I generally let it pass with a warning. We would maintain this posture for a week before moving to the Deo Mang (An Khe) Pass to resume highway duty again, protecting the pass and conducting local patrolling in the area. Our position was near the very top of the pass and we could observe the worst parts of Highway 19 as it traversed through this mountainous winding pass.

This was the 1st week in May and the 1st Cavalry Division had a Change of Command Ceremony with MG John Norton taking command from MG Harry W.O. Kinnard who was moving to the position of Deputy Commander, II Corps. From our position atop the pass we could see the Division conduct a pass in review by most of the helicopters and fixed wing aircraft in the Division during the ceremony. Quite a sight and I'm sure Charlie was wondering "what the hell are these guys up to now." A few days later Norton flew to our position in the pass for a quick visit. It was good to see him; he was the General who had pinned my gold bars on when I earned my commission as a 2nd Lieutenant, Infantry from Officer Candidate School at Fort Benning in December 1964.

Fig 11. MG John Norton, CG 1st Cavalry Division

After a week of duty in the pass we returned to Base Camp and began running platoon size patrols to the West and North of the Camp. These were day insertions and were platoon patrols mainly designed to keep the VC from approaching and getting in mortar or rocket range of the Camp.

On May 20th, the 2nd Platoon was on such a patrol Northwest of Camp Radcliff when I received word to move the platoon quickly to an open area not far from our location and be ready for pickup and movement back to the battalion area. I knew something big must be up. Little did I know that we were about to enter our largest action since my assignment to the Company, but also the biggest action the Company had encountered since mid-December 1965. Shortly thereafter we arrived at the clearing and were picked up by Huey's for transport back to the Mustang Helipad at base camp.

CHAPTER 9

OPERATION CRAZY HORSE – INTO BATTLE

On arrival at the Battalion area we found Martin and the rest of the unit already back in the company area. The troops were frantically working on preparing their gear so we knew whatever was going on we could expect to see action. As the squad leaders got the troops moving to prepare and refit, Martin called the Platoon Leaders and Platoon Sergeants to a briefing. He said a portion of the 1st and 2nd Brigades had already moved to the Vinh Thanh Valley (also known as Happy Valley) and had thwarted an attack by the Viet Cong/PAVN forces on the Special Forces Camp located in the upper valley. They were now heavily engaged in the mountains to the east of the valley. The action had begun on 16th May and our Battalion was being committed to cut off the enemy from fleeing east towards the Soui Ca Valley. As related by Martin, a CIDG Montagnard patrol accompanied by several Sergeants from the Special Forces Camp located in the upper Vinh Thanh Valley (Coordinates BR616605) had ambushed a VC squad in the mountains to the east of the camp and had captured documents, a map of the valley, and a 120mm mortar sight indicating an attack on the camp was imminent. The SF Camp Commander when notified of the find turned to the 1st Cav for help and after evaluating the captured materiels they agreed that an enemy force of undetermined size was located in the mountains overlooking the Special Forces camp.

Based on this evidence MG Norton ordered troops of the 1st Brigade (ABN) into the area hoping to locate and destroy the enemy force before they could withdraw deeper into the mountainous terrain. The first element deployed was B Company, 2/8th Cav (ABN) under the command of Captain J.D. Coleman, who had previously served as the Division Historian and had just assumed command of the company. His order was to conduct a Combat Air Assault into a small clearing on a ridge running from the Valley up into the mountains overlooking the Special Forces compound and to locate and destroy the enemy force should they encounter them. The landing area selected was designated LZ Hereford. Shortly after landing, and as the Company moved up the ridge overlooking the valley in a reconnaissance in force, they became heavily engaged with what they assumed, at first, to be a well-armed and well trained NVA/VC Company size unit. This proved to be a totally false assumption and they quickly realized they were facing at least a battalion of well entrenched enemy soldiers. Their situation became more tenuous as heavy rains prevented use of artillery and air support to the 2/8th and casualties were quickly mounting. Additional forces were requested.

Other Cav units were quickly alerted and A Company 1/12th Cav (ABN) was also airlifted into LZ Hereford, and began moving up the steep ridge to the aid of Coleman and his men. The heavy jungle growth precluded maneuver and restricted the company from deviating from the trail. This complicated things more as the wounded from Coleman's company were coming down the trail for evacuation from the LZ and were running headlong into 1/12th troopers trying to reach the rest of Coleman's company still heavily engaged with the enemy. After several hours they finally were successful and reached the beleaguered company as the enemy force began to withdraw to the east.

In the meantime, the 2/12th Cav assaulted into another small clearing about 3 kilometers Northeast of Hereford designated LZ Horse (BR 693632) in an attempt to encircle and cut off enemy forces from escaping to the east. Horse was located in a valley that ran west to northeast toward the Soui Ca Valley which was quickly named the Denver Trail in keeping with the operation that had now been dubbed "Operation Crazy Horse", after the famed Sioux Chief of the same name.

The Battalion was quickly engaged in running battles with enemy elements to the east of Hereford and to the north of LZ Horse in the triple canopied jungle. The entire 1/8th Battalion (ABN) was then committed, entering the battle at LZ Horse to assist these units and to also destroy enemy forces fleeing from the area.

Martin relayed to us that Chinook helicopters (CH-47s) would soon be inbound and said to have your men quickly refit with additional ammo and rations and be prepared for pickup and transport into the mountains east of the Vinh Thanh Valley. The Battalion Headquarters, along with Alpha, Delta and Charlie Companies had already deployed to LZ Horse around 1300 hours. Alpha and Delta were securing the LZ and Charlie Company had already moved out in support of Bravo Company, 2/12th who were in contact with a strong enemy force to the north of the LZ and to the east of Hill 766, the dominant terrain feature in the area.

Around 1500 hours we moved to the pick-up zone and Bravo Company was lifted by Chinooks from An Khe to a small clearing located in the mountains east of the Vinh Thanh Valley. It was like flying through a chute as we entered the valley with mountain peaks towering high above our route to the LZ, a clearing that we now knew had already been designated LZ Horse and which could accommodate only one CH-47 at a time in the gathering dusk. The 2nd Platoon was the second to land on the LZ at approximately 1600 hours. A light rain/mist was falling as we arrived and the LZ was surrounded by heavily forested mountainous terrain. Sporadic enemy fire was being directed at the LZ from the high ground south of the LZ. Alpha and Delta Companies had already established a defensive perimeter and would return small arms and an occasional mortar round to suppress these fires, but they continued throughout the night. Charlie Company was engaged with an enemy force northeast of the LZ. All in all we knew we were not in a good place.

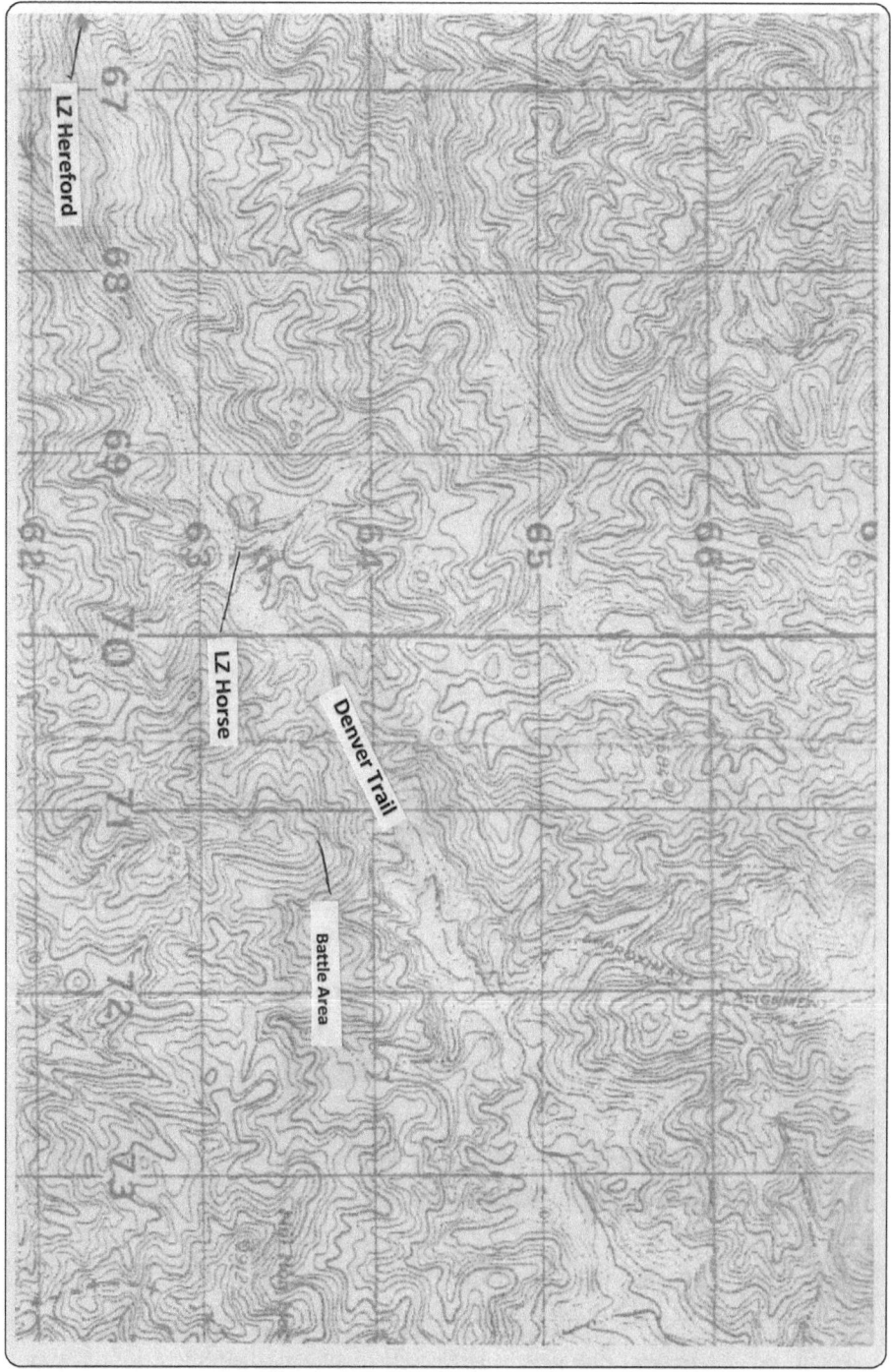

Fig 12. The Denver Trail. LZ Hereford, LZ Horse, and the Battle Area

Once the entire Company was on the ground we were assigned respective areas within the perimeter to set up for the night while Captain Martin headed to the Battalion Command Post for instructions. He soon returned and called the Platoon leaders for a meeting on our next day's mission. Specifically, Bravo Company along with Charlie Company were to link up on the morning of the 21st and generally proceed along the trail and streambed to the northeast of LZ Horse to find, engage and defeat the enemy force suspected of still being in the area. As related by Captain Martin, Charlie Company commanded by Capt. William (Bill) Mozey had arrived earlier that afternoon and had been committed north of the LZ to support B Company, 2/12th who were in contact when they themselves came under fire and an assault by enemy soldiers. They beat back the attack and then set up a perimeter at coordinates BR 697638, about 500 meters northeast of Horse for the night.

The Battalion Commander, Lt Col. Levin Broughton and his staff on LZ Horse, briefed Martin on the operation that was to take place the next day and he in turn briefed his platoon leaders. Bravo Company was to be on the right flank and Charlie Company to the left on the higher ground as we moved to the northeast generally following the small stream and trail that ran the length of the valley. The stream and trail had been designated earlier as the Denver Trail. (Note: In his book "Battles in the Monsoon" Brigadier S.L.A. Marshall stated we arrived on the morning of the 21st via Huey Helicopter lift ships. This was simply not true. We arrived on the afternoon of the 20th as earlier mentioned by Chinook Helicopters. Throughout this narrative I will continue to make reference to and point out other glaring errors made in his narrative of the battle.) Needless to say we spent an uneasy night on the LZ. It was pitch black, rain continued to fall and the enemy continued to snipe at us throughout the night. Whispered conversations could be heard as I checked each of the platoon positions trying to encourage them for the upcoming mission and to alleviate their fears. Even SGT Johnston, the quintessential platoon sergeant, seemed uneasy about what the next day would bring. Bluntly, we all knew contact was imminent and there was nothing we could do about it.

CHAPTER 10

CRAZY HORSE - MOVEMENT TO CONTACT

On May 21st, 1966 Bravo Company moved from the LZ around 0700 hours following the trail and stream to the Northeast as planned. It was already turning hot and was humid even though overcast with mist in the valleys and light fog or clouds at the higher elevations around the LZ. Enemy small arms fire was still occasionally being directed at the perimeter and Alpha Company 1/8th had already moved south/southwest to eliminate this threat. We remained tense and fully expected to make contact at some point during the day. The 2nd Platoon was designated as the lead element and assumed point for the company. I appointed the 2nd squad as lead and the Squad Leader SGT Antonio Lopez appointed Sp4 Milton Parks as point man for the platoon and company. Parks was a large black man whom the platoon trusted fully. The platoon was followed by the remainder of the company who moved in a modified column formation with select individuals out to protect our flanks.

Captain Martin and the Command Group consisting of his two RTOs, Sp4 Jerry Brown and PFC Carrol White, the Company Senior Medic Sp5 Arnold "Arnie" Arellanno, and the Artillery Recon NCO, SGT Robert Clapp, followed the 2nd platoon. (Note: Our Forward Observer, Lt Michael Livengood who normally would have been with us had been returned to his parent unit, the 2/19 Artillery Battalion, and was not with us on the operation. General Marshall in his book has him with us and also had him directing artillery fire later in the day).

The 1st Platoon led by Lt. Bob Crum followed slightly to my right rear on higher ground and was responsible for right flank security. Behind them was the 3rd Platoon commanded by Lt Jerry East. He was charged with the responsibility for rear security and was also designated the company reserve. The mortar platoon commanded by Lt. Bill Hughes would remain on LZ Horse and provide mortar fire in support of our movement as needed. Lt. Crum and I were fairly new, he arriving in mid-February and I in mid-March 1966. Lt. East and Lt. Hughes were old timers having deployed with the Company from Ft. Benning in September 1965.

Charlie Company, 1/8th commanded by Captain Bill Mozey was on our left flank following a parallel ridge on higher ground above the streambed, but to the best of my knowledge no one from Bravo Company ever made visual contact with him or his Company as we began moving.

Fig 13. Captain William Mozey, C Company Commander

Charlie Company, on the other hand, stated they could clearly see us as we moved along the designated route following the stream. They were at least 150 meters to the north of us. (Note: S.L.A. Marshall claims they were located on the bank of the creek. Not so, if they were we would have no trouble spotting them and in fact they would have been intermingled with my platoon). The area along the stream was moderately covered in vegetation with both tall grass and scrub trees. A trail paralleled the stream. Visibility was fair; however, to the left and right the mountains rose quickly from the valley floor and were covered with tall trees, boulders and heavy undergrowth. It felt like the mountainous terrain was closing in on us. We moved slowly and cautiously along or near the stream sensing the enemy was close, but unobserved.

About 500-600 meters northeast of LZ Horse the platoon moved slightly to the left away from the stream and crossed some higher ground. We passed through an area of triple canopy jungle that appeared to have had been the scene of heavy fighting the previous day by either Charlie Company or the company from the 2/12th they had relieved on the 20th. The predominant hill located to the northwest of LZ Horse (according to a map of the area) was Hill 766, which meant the uppermost point of the hill was 766 meters high or roughly 2500 feet above the valley floor. The area we were now crossing (approximately BR700637) was located northeast of LZ Horse and almost due east of Hill 766

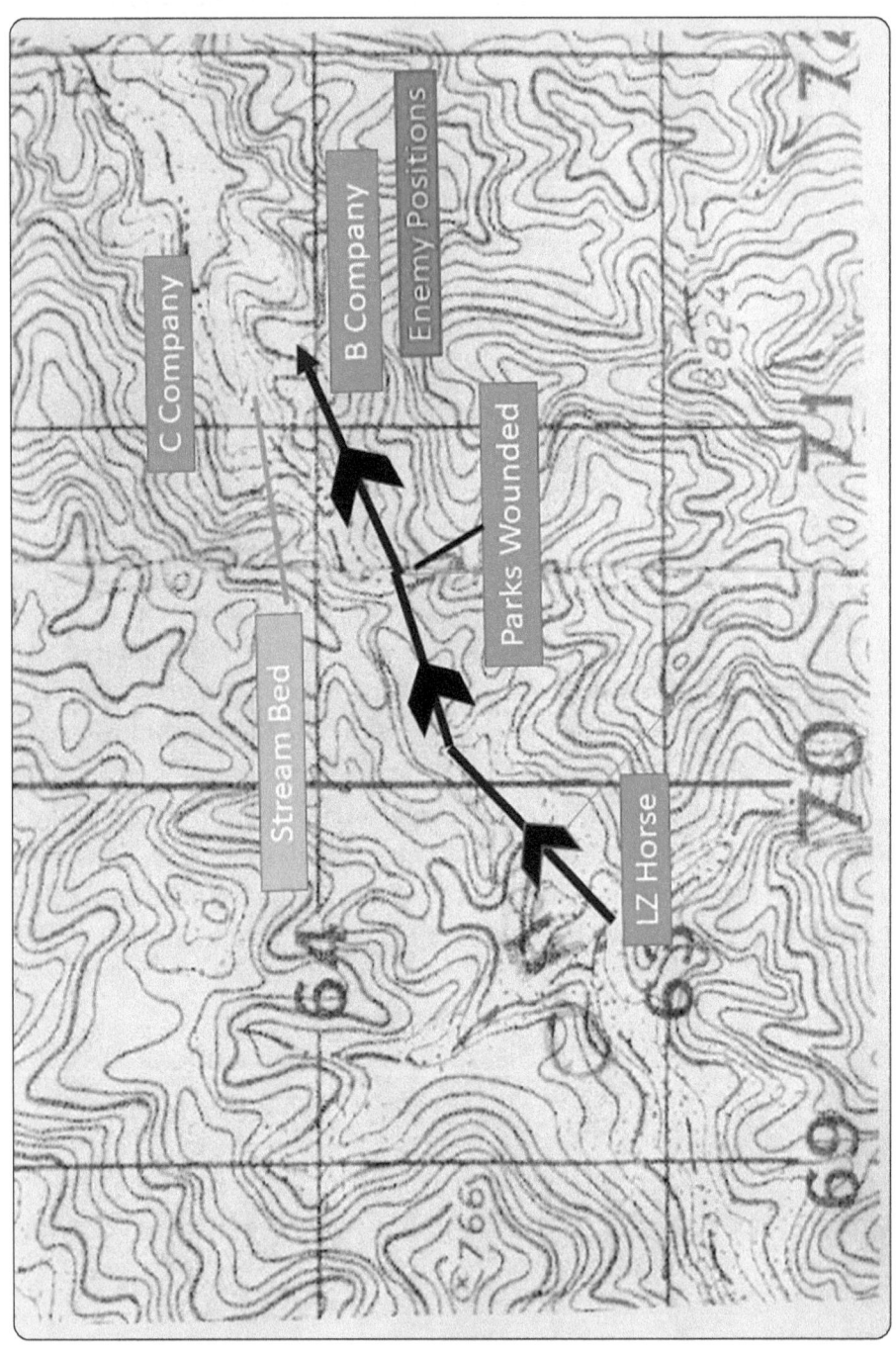

Fig. 14 Movement to Battle

Battle litter (bloody bandages, spent shell casings and miscellaneous items) were strewn throughout an area slightly smaller than a football field and a sickening smell of death permeated everything. Even to this day I still sometimes sense that smell. I also noticed ropes hanging from several tall trees, probably where NVA/VC snipers had been strategically placed to engage any friendly forces entering the area or moving along the streambed.

After passing through we moved down and back toward the stream and continued our move to the northeast. The tension had increased dramatically and we remained on high alert. We still had not made visual contact with Charlie Company nor had we encountered any enemy, but continued to sense they were close.

Around 1000 hours the platoon came to an intersection in the stream (BR706637). The right fork went south while the other, the one we had been following, continued to the northeast. My point squad had started following the stream to the south. Uncertain of which way to proceed I called a halt and radioed Captain Martin, explained the situation, and asked for instructions on which way to proceed. At the same time I ordered my lead squad up a roughly six to 8 foot embankment on our left to take up defensive positions and provide security for the remainder of the platoon which was still spread along the original streambed. The tip of this embankment was in reality the point of a finger ridge flowing from the south/southeast down to the streambed. As the squad moved into position at the top of the bank it came under fire and Sp4 Parks was shot in the right hip. The squad immediately returned fire toward the suspected enemy position and the unknown size enemy force withdrew. (Note: In his book "Battles in the Monsoon" BG Marshall says no blood was drawn during this short encounter. Again, he was wrong in his description of the battle).

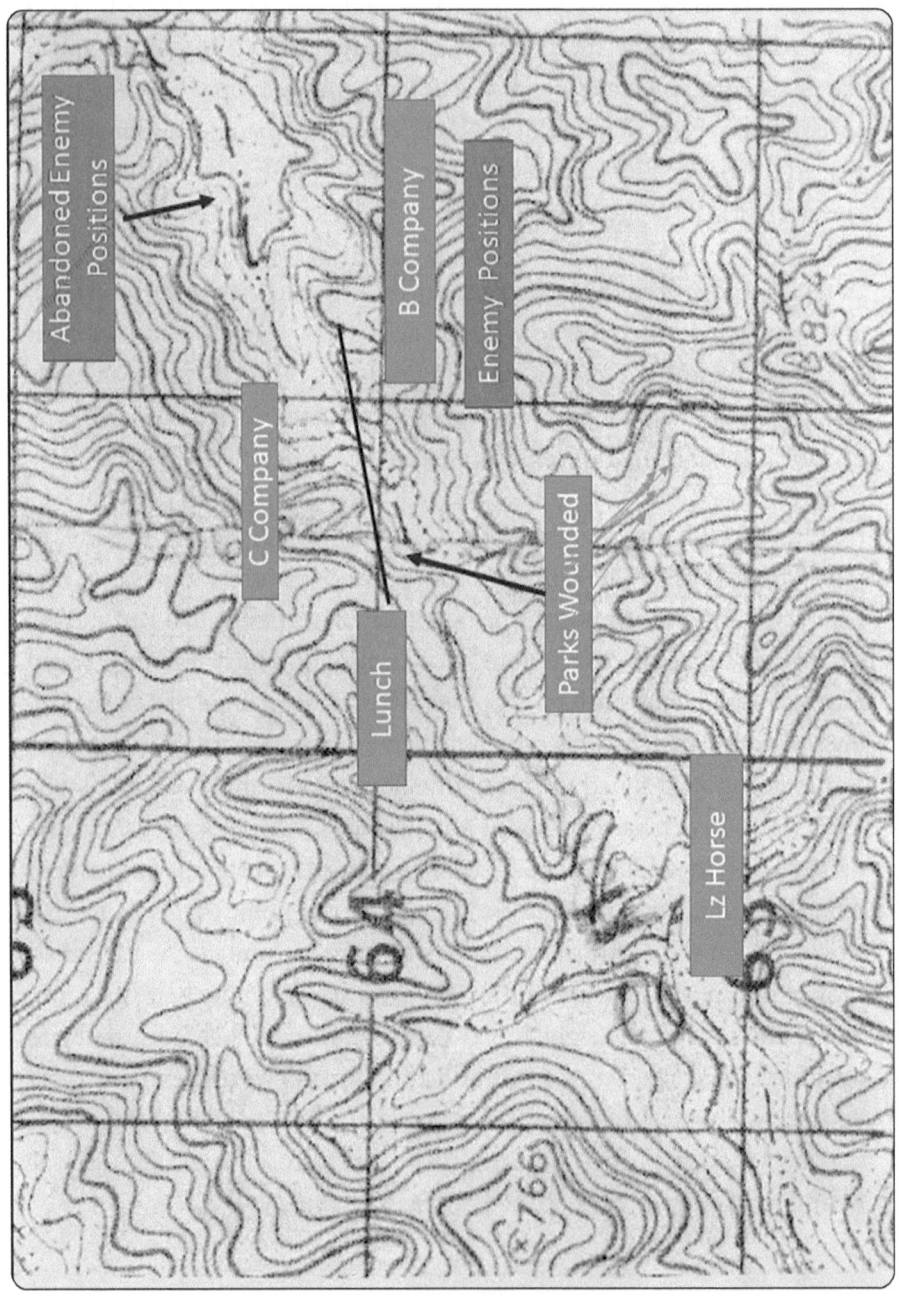

Fig 15. Parks wounded and area of Battle

And the Tears Flowed

Several members of the platoon pulled Parks back to the protection of the streambed where the platoon medic began working on his wound to stop the bleeding and to also prevent Parks from going into shock. The remainder of the platoon took up a defensive posture as he worked. Capt. Martin, the command group, and 1st Sergeant Ray "Top" Poynter joined me in the streambed. Poynter organized a litter for Parks, made from two poles and a poncho, and filled out a casualty report while the senior medic, began assisting Alston with Parks. I then designated a squad, led by Sergeant Dewey Underwood, to escort Parks back to LZ Horse since there were no suitable landing sites in the immediate vicinity of our location allowing evacuation by helicopter. This entire action took approximately 30 minutes to complete. Needless to say we were all now as tight as drums knowing for sure there were enemy soldiers in the area. I also worried for the safety of the squad moving back to LZ Horse, since they would be moving back through an area where heavy fighting had taken place over several days prior and there remained a distinct possibility that enemy forces may still be located along the route back to the LZ. This however, was not the case and they were able to return to the Horse unscathed. Parks was then evacuated to the 15th Med Battalion at Camp Radcliffe. The squad who littered Parks back to Horse remained at the LZ resulting in the 2nd platoon now being at an overall strength of 20-25 men vice the standard 46 men in a rifle platoon.

With the evacuation complete and after consultation with the Company Commander, we concluded the enemy position was probably an outpost for a larger force. Martin ordered the Company to again begin moving to the northeast and parallel to the original stream with the 2nd Platoon still leading. We were now about 50-100 meters south of the stream traversing over the ridge where the enemy had fired on us. We crossed this ridge (or finger), which flowed from higher ground in the south towards the stream, and then moved down and through a draw, crossed another finger ridge and draw, and then approached a third finger ridge. Our movement was slow, measured, and cautious. As the platoon moved up this next ridge we found enemy positions that, without question, had recently been occupied by an NVA/VC force of unknown strength, but estimated to be at least company size. Cooking fires were still smoldering and warm rice was scattered around the fires. A heavily traveled trail 6 to 8 feet wide ran through the center of the finger and led down to the stream. As I recall this ridge or finger was about 800-1000 meters from the earlier firing incident and what I now estimated to be about 2500 meters from LZ Horse.

At this juncture Captain Martin called a halt to our movement and told the platoon leaders to establish a perimeter on this finger ridge so he could make contact and meet with C Company's Commander, Captain Bill Mozey near the stream. It was around 1230hrs in the afternoon. On Martin's instructions I moved the 2nd Platoon to cover the south and eastern side of the finger, covering the southern portion of the trail with one of my two machine guns, guessing the enemy would have withdrawn up the trail to the higher ground and could pose a threat should they decide to attack down the ridge. The other gun I placed covering the draw to the northeast. I could see yet another ridge to the east/northeast with another draw between our position and that ridge. Close to the stream this draw was fairly open; but, toward the higher ground it was heavily vegetated, covered with large boulders, and the back of the draw was extremely steep. Lt Crum's Platoon tied in to mine and covered a portion of the north and east side of the perimeter overlooking the draw and the streambed. Lt East's platoon covered the remainder of the perimeter by linking in with both platoons and covering the area to the west which we had just traversed.

Charlie Company was now positioned across the stream to our north and were higher up on a hill mass, somewhat parallel to and overlooking our perimeter. Martin advised us to eat lunch during the halt as we might not have an opportunity to do so later. He then met and conferred with Mozey near the streambed so they could plan their next moves and preclude any confusion by either company of our locations when we resumed the assigned mission.

And the Tears Flowed

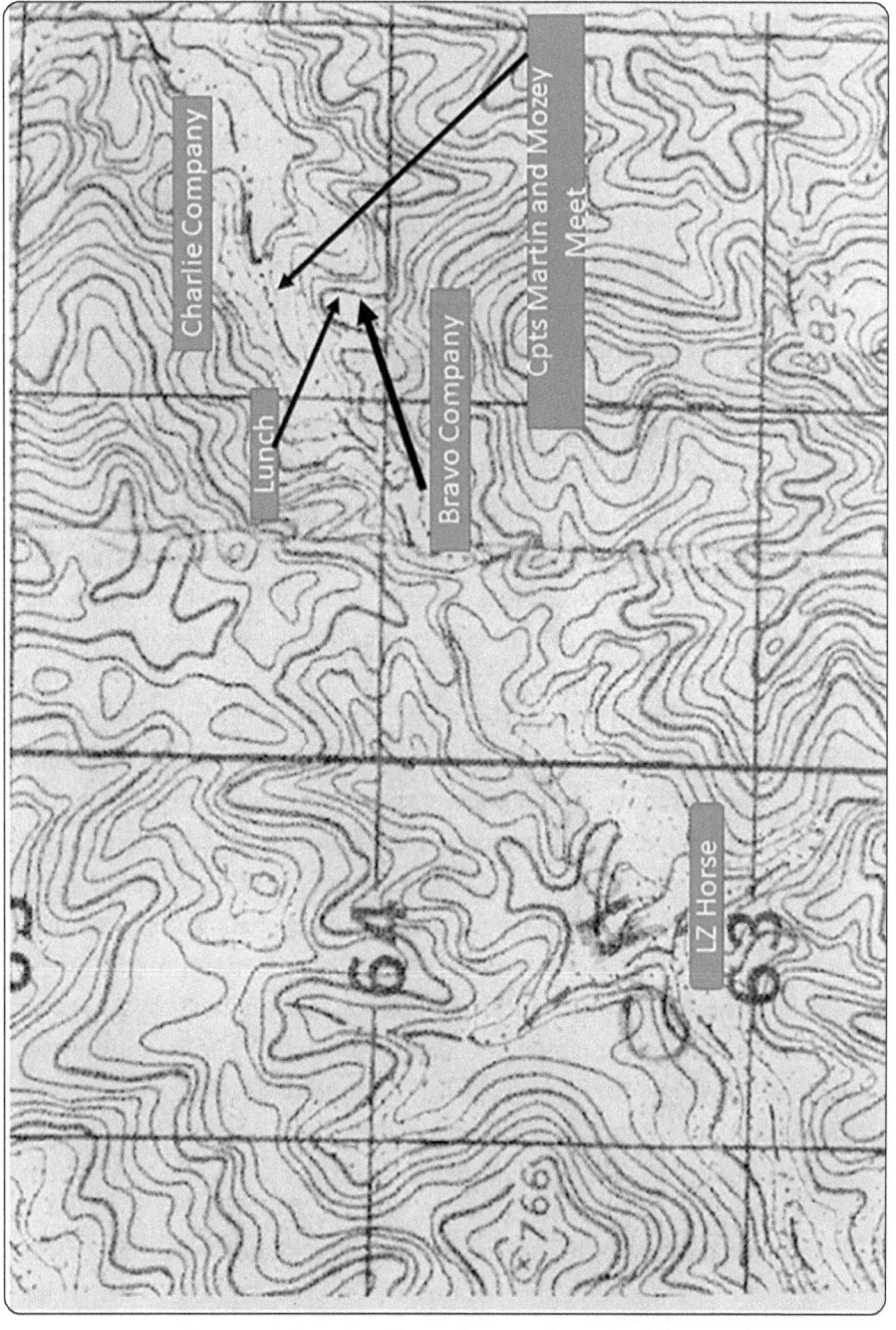

Fig 16. Lunch/CPTs Martin and Mozey Meet

During the break my machine gun crew covering the trail to the South spotted 2 or 3 enemy soldiers about 75 yards from their position moving down the trail towards our perimeter; however, before they could engage, the enemy soldiers turned and vanished into the triple canopy jungle to the east. I immediately reported this to Martin and also alerted the other platoon leaders. When Martin returned from his meeting he called the platoon leaders to the Command Group location in the center of the perimeter where he again briefed us on our mission. We would continue our movement to the northeast generally paralleling the stream and attempt to make contact and then destroy any NVA/VC force in the area. We would continue as before with the 2nd Platoon in the lead, followed by the Command Group, the 1st Platoon, and then the 3rd Platoon. Charlie Company would monitor our initial movement from their positions across the streambed and provide fire support if needed. They would then move parallel to our company once we reached the next finger ridge. I remained uneasy since we would be traversing terrain parallel to the direction the three enemy soldiers had taken.

According to Martin he had also noted unoccupied enemy bunkers on Charlie Company's side of the stream and Mozey had Lt Jon Williams and his platoon move in and occupy these bunkers which gave them a good view of the area. The positions would provide Charlie Company a good view of both the stream and the draw as Bravo Company traversed the area toward the next finger ridge. Mozey had his 1st Platoon, commanded by Lt Patrick Greiner, remain on the high ground to the North of the stream and had his 3rd Platoon, commanded by Lt Frank Vavrek, move slightly closer to the stream to observe our position on the finger ridge where we had eaten lunch and to cover us if the enemy should initiate contact. Martin and Mozey were uneasy and both felt we were about to make contact they just did not know where or when.

At approximately 1400 hours my platoon moved off the finger ridge, swung away from the stream, and moved slightly to the right. The Command Group followed. Our movement was cautious and painstakingly slow since we had spotted enemy soldiers in the area.

In addition, the draw was heavily vegetated and strewn with large boulders. Tall trees covered the area further impeding our movement. The humidity and heat had increased considerately also slowing our movement. Tensions were high among the men of the 2nd platoon as we moved toward the next finger ridge. The 1st Platoon, instead of following the route taken by my platoon and the Command Group, swung more to the left toward the stream which put them in a more open and less densely covered area. This made their movement easier, but also made them much more vulnerable to the attack that was forthcoming.

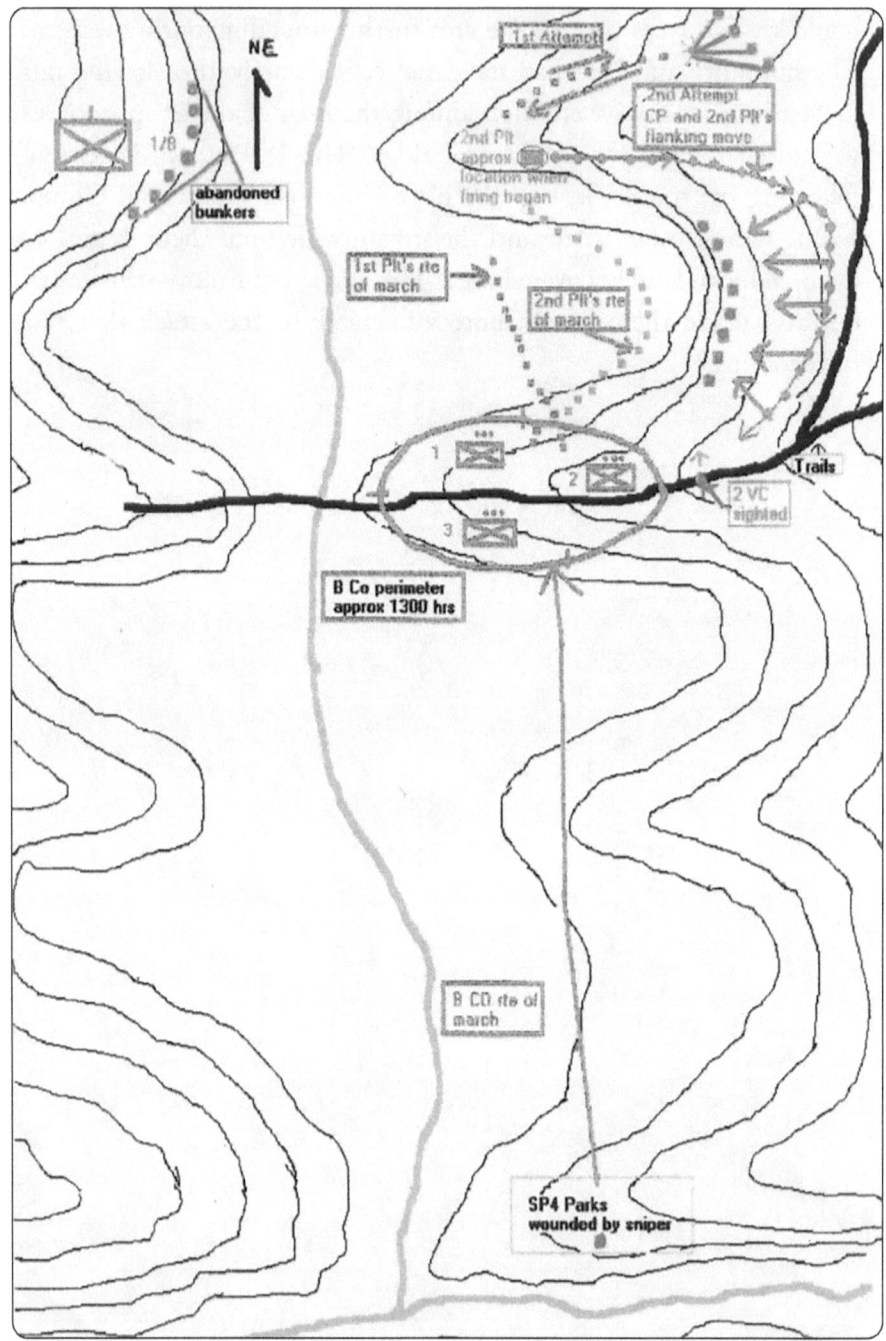

Fig 17. Hand Drawn Map of Battle

CHAPTER 11

CRAZY HORSE - CONTACT

As the 2nd Platoon finally reached and began moving across the next finger ridge, a violent and sustained burst of NVA/VC heavy weapons fire erupted behind us and was directed at the remainder of the company following my platoon. The fire came from well-concealed enemy positions and bunkers to my right rear and from the steep ridge at the back of the draw. At least two 50-caliber and several 30-caliber machine guns, as well as AK-47 and SKS assault rifles were raining accurate and deadly fire on Bob Crum's 1st Platoon, who had taken casualties immediately from the initial burst of fire, and were now pinned down. Jerry East's 3rd Platoon, which had just begun their movement into the draw, was also receiving heavy fire and were unable to move from the finger ridge. Without question the NVA had initiated an almost perfect ambush on the 1st and 3rd Platoons, even though the 3rd had not suffered any casualties and had basically isolated my platoon and the Command Group from the rest of the company. It was now close to 1500 hours.

After the initial shock I realized no enemy fire was being directed at the 2nd Platoon. CPT Martin and his command group had also made the same finger ridge as my platoon and he immediately began assessing the situation. By radio he asked if I could maneuver against the enemy positions at the top of the draw who were continuing to direct heavy fire at the rest of the company. I said I would try and in turn ordered the platoon to move on line and begin moving up the finger towards the enemy positions in an effort to flank their positions. Despite what had been taught during tactics training at The Infantry School, Fort Benning, Georgia to immediately charge the enemy positions and attempt a breakout, I instructed the platoon to stay low and to crawl up the finger toward the entrenched enemy force. I still did not know the size of the enemy force, but knew it was substantial from the number of machine guns and small arms firing on the rest of the company. I suspected at least a reinforced company or an even larger force.

As we pushed up the finger the platoon had still not drawn any fire; however, as we neared the upper portion of the ridge near the military crest a young black soldier on the left flank yelled "there's a GI up here." Looking to my front and left I spotted a fully armed NVA soldier in a khaki uniform and pith helmet commonly associated with the NVA Army standing about 30 yards away. He appeared to be looking for us which, I assume, he though we would have charged up the finger. Several of the platoon members immediately took him under fire and he dropped to the ground. In turn the platoon was greeted with a hail of fire from the top and the left side of the ridge. Apparently the NVA/VC force had established a second ambush position to prevent us from attacking the enemy positions that were firing on the remainder of the company, but had unknowingly left a gap between their positions. Another possibility was they were moving to reinforce their comrades who had sprung the ambush. Surprisingly none of the platoon members were hit although I could hear bullets whipping past my head, impacting trees, kicking up dirt, and especially snapping branches over our heads. You could actually hear the snap of bullets as they went by. This is often the case when a force occupies a position above the force below them, they tend to fire high, although some rounds without a doubt were hitting the ground to our immediate front, throwing dirt in our faces.

Concerned we were now facing a second ambush or additional enemy forces moving in to destroy us, I ordered the platoon to withdraw back towards the stream to figure out what other possible plans of action were available to us. During this retrograde movement we found the

Company Command Group hunkered behind several large trees in a defiladed position about 50-75 yards from the stream. As I moved toward the Captain, I looked back towards the 1st Platoon's positions in the draw and could see Sergeant Gerald Hoover, a squad leader in the 1st Platoon, lying dead about 15 yards from my location.

Fig 18. SGT Gerald Hoover

CPT Martin, in a calm and steady voice, stated that Hoover had just reported Lt. Crum was dead as were a number of others in the 1st Platoon just prior to Hoover himself being struck in the chest by an enemy round that killed him almost instantly.

Martin returned fire on the enemy soldier who had fired the shot that killed Hoover and in turn killed him at a distance of some 15-20 feet. The CO then said that Lt East and the 3rd Platoon was reporting they were still occupying the ridge, for the most part, where we had eaten lunch and could not move due to heavy fire from the enemy positions above him. I told Martin we had attempted to flank the enemy positions who were firing on the other two platoons, but were unsuccessful inasmuch as the platoon had drawn fire from what appeared to be well concealed positions to our front and left as we moved up the finger. I also told him we still had not received any fire from our right and that it appeared there may be a gap in the NVA/VC positions that could be breached.

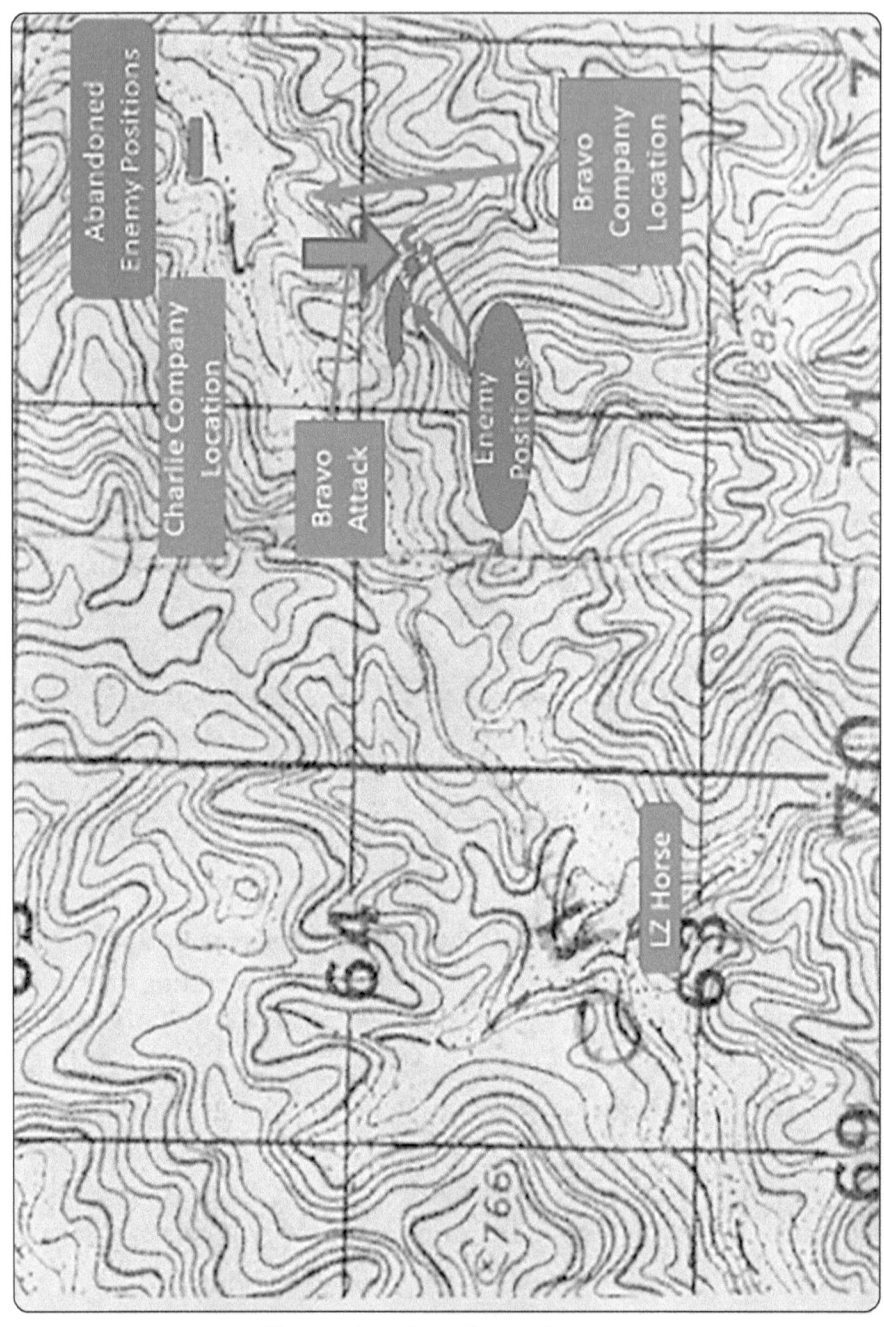

Fig 19. Assault on Enemy Positions

Martin made a quick on the spot decision and in a steady and calm voice said, "That's where we are going to attack." Sp4 Jerry Brown relayed the decision to Battalion HQs on LZ Horse. My platoon now accompanied by the Command Group again began moving up the finger, but this time maneuvered to the right side of the ridge and towards the draw where 1st Platoon remained trapped. A heavy rain had begun falling in sheets at the outset of our move and the light was fading quickly due to this downpour and the tall trees around us which virtually blocked out the sky. Charlie Company and our 3rd Platoon aided our movement at the request of Captain Martin by placing a heavy volume of fire on the NVA/VC force located near the top of the ridge where the initial enemy fire came from. This concentrated fire evidently caused the enemy to stay down and probably prevented any reinforcement of the main ambush positions; however, the enemy force did continue to fire on the 1st and 3rd Platoons, but at a much reduced volume. Additionally, Captain Martin had requested and received operational control of a platoon led by Lt Frank Vavrek from Charlie Company to fill the gap created when the critically injured 1st platoon survivors and wounded began withdrawing towards the 3rd Platoon and Charlie Company elements.

Fig 20. LT Frank Vavrek, 3rd Plt Charlie Company

These moves allowed us to move undetected past the enemy bunkers positioned along the military crest near the top of the ridge.

Meanwhile, our 3rd Platoon, who remained pinned down on the finger ridge where we ate lunch, and Vavrek's Platoon jointly repulsed an enemy force, of at least platoon size, who were attempting to flank their positions from the Southwest. Poynter and PSG Robinson also encountered enemy soldiers and also successfully neutralized them although Robinson's M-16 took a round in the magazine effectively putting his rifle out of action. Poynter shot and killed 3 of the attacking enemy soldiers halting the attack on their position.

Martin during this time called for Charlie Company to shift their fire to the top of the hill mass above our location and on suspected enemy routes of movement into the area. Mozey meanwhile also ordered Lt Jon Williams to send part of his platoon down to the stream to evacuate our wounded to his location near the top of the ridge to our North.

On successfully reaching a position slightly below the top of the hill, the 2nd platoon and the Command Group turned right paralleling a heavily used trail behind the main enemy positions. Platoon Sergeant James L. Johnson tripped over some communications wires running from the enemy positions below us to an unknown location above us, in all likelihood the headquarters element of the enemy force. We now knew we were facing more than a random meeting and a much larger force than we previously thought. It was obvious the NVA/VC force we were fighting had prepared the battlefield wisely with communications wires laid and bunkers built overlooking the Denver Trail to stop anyone from using it to move against them. Johnson cut the wires thereby severing any communications between the enemy command post and the forces now below us. I told Johnson and Sergeant Arsenio Lujan, along with several of his squad, to take up security positions to prevent any reinforcements from approaching from the south or east. The remainder of my platoon deployed on line behind the dug-in enemy bunker line below us. The Command Group also deployed along this same line with Martin, his RTOs, the company medic and the Artillery Recon Sergeant to the right of my position. Sp4 William Goode, the platoon mortar forward observer, was to my left and one rifle squad led by Sergeant Leroy Christian were deployed just beyond him. Sergeant Antonio Lopez' rifle squad was to my right just past the Command Group. The weapons squad's machine gun crews were interspersed with both assaulting rifle squads. By my estimate the total strength of our assault force including the Command Group was no more than 30 men, if that, since one of my squads had transported Sp4 Parks back to LZ Horse earlier. Once we were deployed Martin ordered the attack on the enemy positions below us.

CHAPTER 12

CRAZY HORSE - THE ASSAULT

As we began moving down toward the enemy force below us they apparently became aware they had been flanked and were now attempting to reposition weapons and men to meet our attack. We immediately took them under fire and started inflicting heavy casualties on them. I moved behind a large tree and told PFC Allen Ritter, my acting RTO, to stay behind me and the tree; however, he stepped out to engage an NVA soldier trying to escape the deadly fire. An enemy machine gun opened fire on our position wounding Ritter in the leg just above the knee. I spotted the machine gun as I and the platoon medic pulled Ritter back to the safety of the tree. Alston, the medic, began working on him to stop the bleeding and to bandage the wound while under intense enemy fire.

Fig 21. PFC Alan Ritter

I estimated the gun was 15 to 20 yards from my position, well camouflaged but no overhead cover, and was located just to the left side of a heavily traveled trail which led down towards the stream. (Note: This trail turned out to be the same trail that ran down the finger where we had stopped for lunch). Realizing this position was a direct threat to the assault and, if not neutralized, would jeopardize our movement on the bunker complex. Without hesitation I pulled a grenade from my harness, pulled the pin, released the handle, waited two counts and then threw it at the machine gun position. Not a brilliant move on my part since grenades have a mind of their own and sometimes explode at two seconds vice 5 seconds; however, in this case luck was with me and it exploded just above the enemy position. I sprinted quickly downhill and engaged the three or four NVA soldiers occupying the position. The gunner, although dazed and seriously wounded, was attempting to reach for the machine gun when I shot him point blank. The other occupants were either dead from the grenade blast or from the shots I sprayed on reaching their position. Looking down the trail I saw another NVA soldier moving up the trail carrying additional boxes of machine gun ammunition evidently with the intent to re-supply the position I had just neutralized. I fired twice hitting him center mass, meaning I shot him in the chest, and he fell on the spot. He carried an almost brand new SKS assault rifle slung across his back. I retrieved the rifle and began moving towards a bunker to the right of the trail motioning for the squads on my right and left to continue the attack down the finger. I tossed another grenade through the rear entrance of the bunker, took cover until it exploded then sprayed the bunker with my M-16. I don't know if I killed the occupants in the bunker, but there was no further fire or voices from it so I assumed I had and they would no longer present a threat to us. I and Martin continued to urge the platoon forward. They did and they performed brilliantly. To the right and left I could see the remainder of the platoon and the Command Group advancing on and through the bunker complex, destroying bunkers as they progressed down the finger toward the friendly platoons below. I specifically recalled Sp4 William Goode and the squad to my left throwing grenades, firing their M-16s, M-79 grenade launchers, and machine guns as they moved toward and through the bunkers neutralizing each as they moved past.

Sp4 Douglas Asher remembered firing his M-79 directly at the head of an enemy combatant killing him instantly. Asher also remembers moving down the trail as one of the last men in the attack formation. He remembered it getting dark and the heavy falling rain, which made it almost impossible to see. He also saw a communications wire running down the trail which had been cut. While lying near the trail he saw another individual moving down the trail, mistook him for one of the Hispanics in the platoon, and asked "what are you doing", before noting he had a pistol in his hand. Asher then related the individual looked terrified, but then raised the pistol and pointed at Asher's face and pulled the trigger. Luckily the pistol misfired and Asher, now realizing it was an NVA soldier, fired his M-79 at the individual and yelled at several of the platoon members near him to "get him of me." They immediately took the enemy soldier under fire, but in the diminishing light, missed and he vanished into the darkness.

Off to my right I could see Captain Martin, the command group, and Sergeant Lopez and his squad doing the same, attacking bunkers and enemy soldiers fleeing from the battle. Martin took out a least one sniper in the trees to our front and then personally attacked several of the bunkers that had been firing on our 1st and 3rd Platoons. I also observed Lopez shoot another NVA soldier moving up a trail towards his and Martin's position. Although I did not personally witness any other platoon members individual actions, there is little question they were inflicting heavy casualties on the NVA force, since they were no longer returning fire at either the assault force or the friendly forces at the bottom of the ridge and enemy soldiers were being shot as they attempted to flee the area.

It was now approaching 2000 hours and the heavy downpour continued to fall. Full darkness had moved in and flares, called in by Charlie Company's artillery forward observer, guided us as we neared the bottom of the finger ridge where we were met by Lt East's 3rd Platoon and Vavrek's 3nd platoon. Captain Martin directed both platoon leaders to begin evacuating the remaining wounded and dead from our 1st Platoon across the streambed and into the safety of Charlie Company's defensive perimeter which had been established on the opposite ridge. He turned and asked me and my platoon to provide security for the two platoons as they conducted the evacuation. There still remained a concern that the NVA would reorganize and resume their attack, although this did not occur. Martin then formed a small search party from my platoon and began scouring the draw for any dead or missing warriors who had not yet been recovered, a daunting task in the heavy rain and darkness.

CHAPTER 13

CRAZY HORSE – CONSOLIDATION AND CLEAN UP

The search and evacuation lasted several hours as the wounded and the dead were transported across the steam and up the trail into Charlie Company's perimeter on the high ground to our North. This alone proved to be a difficult and backbreaking task as the trail leading to their perimeter had become a muddy morass from the heavy rainfall. Troopers would make their way five or ten feet up the trail with the wounded and dead and then lose their footing and slide back down the trail six feet or more. We eventually had to use ropes to help negotiate our way up the trail. The movement was finally completed after midnight when the Command Group and my Platoon closed on the perimeter. 1st Sergeant Poynter met me as I entered the security of Charlie Company's position and told me Ritter, my RTO, had not made it. He said Ritter died shortly after he carried him into the perimeter. The news was devastating and deeply saddening inasmuch as the medics and others had been able to keep him alive and then transport him to the safety of Charlie Company only to have him expire just as they reached the perimeter. He was the only casualty with the assault force.

The wounded and dead were moved to the center of the perimeter and the medics from both companies were working feverishly on the wounded. A company head count was taken and it was discovered

And the Tears Flowed

Lt. Crum and Private Angel Rodriguez were still missing. Captain Martin, after conferring with Captain Mozey, decided a search would be conducted in the morning since all reports from the remainder of the 1st Platoon said Crum and Rodriguez both had been killed and a search in the dark may prove fruitless and could be extremely dangerous.

Captain Martin after thanking me and the platoon then directed me to move the 2nd Platoon further along the ridge to the northeastern end of the perimeter and take up positions in case of further attacks during the night or in the morning. Just moving the platoon further up the ridge to this designated area proved to be a task in itself with the muddy conditions and the fact all of us were totally exhausted. This, coupled with a young soldier freezing up and refusing to move any further, added to my frustration. After much cojoling and outright threats of bodily harm he finally was persuaded to join the other members of the platoon in moving to our designated position in the perimeter. I instructed the squad leaders to have the men dig in as best they could and have three men man each of these defensive positions, making sure the flanking positions were tied into the positions already established by Charlie Company and our 3rd Platoon. I also instructed each position to keep one man on alert and that they eat what rations they still had and get as much rest as possible over the remainder of the night. I do not think most of them slept at all, even though exhausted. I positioned the platoon headquarters just behind the extended perimeter and notified Captain Martin when we were finally in position. I then walked to each of the platoon's defensive positions and personally thanked each of the men for the outstanding performance and discipline they displayed during the conduct of the assault.

With that accomplished I moved back to the Platoon CP sat down, with my back against a large tree, totally exhausted, and began to cry unabashedly as the totality of our actions during the battle overwhelmed me. AS THE TEARS FLOWED I thought back to the loss of the brave men in the company whom I had come to respect during the short time I had been with the Company. The loss of Lt Bob Crum especially hit hard. We had spoken many times and were planning as brothers-in-arms to serve the year together. The battle dashed those hopes in a devastating and totally brutal manner. Ritter's death was also heartbreaking, bitter in that my Medic had worked so hard to save him, only to see him pass as we finally reached the friendly confines of the perimeter established by Charlie Company. I also reflected on what, if anything, I could have done differently but drew a blank. Other than failing to detect the ambush all the men of the 2nd Platoon and the Command Group had performed superbly and heroically in breaking and defeating a numerically superior enemy force who had, without a doubt, prepared the battlefield to his advantage, but were still defeated by the willpower and determination of these brave men.

It was now May 22nd and the artillery units who had been repositioned earlier now continued to fire illumination rounds throughout the night. The rain continued to fall heavily through the night and although there was occasional sporadic rifle fire there were no probes attempted on the perimeter to my knowledge. The enemy force had evidently fled the area to lick their wounds.

(Note: BG S.L.A. Marshall, the "unofficial" Historian of the US Army, wrote of this Battle. In his book titled "Battles in the Monsoon" he wrote that PFC David Dolby, a machine gunner in the 1st Platoon who was later awarded the Medal of Honor, basically single handedly routed the dug in enemy force taking out three machine gun positions, directing others in the platoon after the platoon leader had been killed, and calling Lt Livengood, the Artillery Forward Observer, to call in artillery and air strikes on the enemy positions.

Fig 22. PFC David C Dolby, Medal of Honor Recipient

This simply did not and could not have happened. Lt Livengood was not with the Company during the battle; he had returned to his parent unit, the 2/19th Artillery. SGT Jim Flagg was the artillery recon sergeant that day and he had told Martin that the 2/19 Artillery Battery supporting us was relocating at the onset of the battle, and were unable to support us with fire. In short we had no artillery support during most of the battle. When it did become available it was used to fire on likely enemy avenues of approach to the battle area and later provided illumination as we moved to the safety of Charlie Company's perimeter. Heavy rains also precluded the use of air support, even though Marshall cites the use of air, specifically Aerial Rocket Artillery (ARA). Had air or artillery been used it would have killed or wounded more of us than the enemy since they were in bunkers with overhead cover, a privilege not available to us in the triple canopied jungle. Marshall also cited Mozey calling in 60 mm mortar fire from LZ Horse. Again this did not happen and if it had it would be 81mm mortars, not 60mm. We didn't have '60s.) Marshall, when he interviewed Dolby and several others soldiers from the 1st platoon after the battle did not include any officers or senior NCOs while he conducted the interview that led to the citation awarding Dolby the medal).

(Note: At approximately the same time our battle took place, the NVA/VC attacked and overwhelmed the mortar platoon from Charlie Company, 1/12 Cavalry at LZ Hereford some 2500 meters West of LZ Horse. The platoon had a strength of 20 men when they came under attack and only 5 survived the onslaught. A reporter/photographer from LOOK Magazine, Sam Castan, had joined the platoon that morning and was among those killed on the LZ. I believe this action, given the severity of basically losing an entire platoon, drew the Division's and Brigade's major attention, therefore overshadowing our battle that raged about 5000 meters further east. Whether it was a coordinated attack to coincide with the attack on our element remains to be seen. The enemy could not have known there would be only a platoon on Hereford, but they may have deduced Charlie Company, 1/12th was moving toward LZ Hereford and they were preparing to attack them. This is of course only supposition on my part, but I feel is worthy at least some consideration).

CHAPTER 14

CRAZY HORSE – THE AFTERMATH

As the morning of the 22nd broke, helicopters flew over the perimeter and dropped much needed supplies, including chainsaws that allowed the troops in the perimeter to open a clearing large enough so the wounded and dead could be evacuated by baskets winched down from a CH-47 Chinook helicopter. The wounded were lifted out first, then the dead. Captured equipment and documents were evacuated last. Charlie Company accomplished most of this effort under a still falling rain. My platoon, along with the remainder of Bravo Company, took this opportunity to rest, clean weapons, and resupply with ammunition and rations delivered by the Chinooks when they arrived.

Captain Mozey, guided by Privates David Dolby and Kenneth Fernandez from the 1st Platoon of Bravo Company, returned to the site of initial contact with a platoon from Charlie Company. They found and recovered the bodies of Lt. Crum and PFC Angel Rodriguez and evacuated the bodies to the safety of the perimeter. The total killed in the battle now numbered ten; seven from the 1st Platoon, Sp4 Alan Ritter from my platoon, and two from Vavrek's platoon. There were also 15 wounded, again mostly from the 1st Platoon who had taken the brunt of the ambush.

Charlie Company then returned to the top of the ridge where the NVA had initiated the battle from the well-constructed and concealed bunkers. According to Mozey, they found 55 NVA/VC bodies including the body of a senior NVA commander and a Chinese Advisor, in one of the bunkers. This from Mozey who recovered a photo from the body of the Chinese Officer in full dress uniform with his family. They also found numerous blood trails and battle litter leading away from the area indicating the NVA had suffered even more casualties as they withdrew. (Note: The NVA/VC normally tried to recover the bodies of their fallen. In this case they did not, indicating the damage to them were devastating). They made no contact during their search of the area and then returned to the ridge where Bravo and the remainder of Charlie Company still manned the perimeter with additional weapons and materials they had found. Evacuation of all materials was completed later that day by helicopter and both companies remained in position for another night before moving their separate ways on May 23rd.

Bravo Company was ordered back to LZ Horse by a circuitous overland route through the mountainous terrain and jungle with the 2nd Platoon again moving as point for the company. During the move we discovered a major NVA/VC base camp and several graves near another stream to the west of the battle site. The encampment was capable of holding at least a battalion size element, complete with latrines, cooking areas dug into the banks above the stream in such a manner as to diffuse the smoke, and sleeping areas; however, we made no further contact with any enemy soldiers in the area and returned to LZ Horse without further incident. The Company was then air lifted to LZ Colt in the southern portion of the Crazy Horse Area of Operations where we assumed defensive perimeter duty with other units of the battalion on a forward artillery base along with a unit from the Republic of Korea Army's White Horse Division. The perimeter was probed several times by small enemy units and we were continually fired on by snipers at the new location.

CHAPTER 15

CRAZY HORSE – LZ COLT AND CHANGE OF COMMAND

I was called to the Company Command Post by Captain Martin the day after arriving at Colt. He introduced me to a new lieutenant, Robert Heath, who had been assigned to the company to replace Lt. Crum. Since my platoon was preparing to move out on a patrol to the west and south of the LZ he assigned Heath to me, much like I had been assigned to LT Hughes when I first arrived. I felt honored that Roy felt confident enough in me to take a new Lieutenant under wing and evaluate him on his capabilities in the field. I turned to Heath and pointed to where my platoon CP was located in the scraggly underbrush and told him assemble his gear and meet me at my CP. He finally showed up, but not with his M-16 but rather an M-72 LAW, a single shot antitank weapon. I and a few others from my command group looked at him incredulously. Finally, I was able to say in a not to friendly voice, "where the hell is your M-16?" His response almost floored me, "I am a Lieutenant; soon to be platoon leader, there is no need for me to carry an M-16, I am quite comfortable with my .45 pistol and this antitank weapon." I could see some of the soldiers rolling their eyes, trying to hide the snickers and laughs at this explanation. I, on the other hand was starting a slow burn. In no uncertain terms I told him to beat feet back to where his rifle was and return post haste. If he didn't he would not be part of the patrol. Needless to say he moved out smartly and returned with his rifle and we finally were able to begin the patrol of our assigned area. It turned out LT Heath was an armor officer and ready to accept the job of an infantry platoon leader, a job he was not well suited or trained for, but a job he eventually gave his best effort and, in my opinion, did reasonably well, at least for the short time I knew him.

We continued to patrol aggressively around the LZ in platoon size elements and during one of these patrols Captain Martin, while guiding the 2nd platoon from a helicopter to one of the sniper locations, was seriously wounded in the leg by the sniper who fired a snap shot at the helicopter. The pilot knew the wound was serious and flew Roy immediately to the 15th Med Hospital in Qui Nhon for life saving medical attention. This move without question saved Roy's life. Roy was eventually evacuated back to the United States and never returned to the company. His loss was felt immediately not only by my platoon, but by the entire company and battalion. Sadly we never located the sniper nor did we make any contact with any enemy forces during the remainder of the patrol.

Captain Gerrell (Gerry) V. Plummer was flown in from Battalion Rear and took command of the company following Roy's evacuation and I believe he knew he had big shoes to fill. Plummer, also a former commander of the Golden Knights Parachute Team, unlike Captain Martin was straight laced and uptight, but with a dry sense of humor. Basically, he was a no nonsense type who expected his orders to be carried out without question. Still all in all he was likeable and a good commander. We continued to conduct squad and platoon size patrols for several days in the area surrounding LZ Colt with little results other than the occasional sniper fire.

Fig 23. Captain Gerrell (Gerry) Plummer

CHAPTER 16

BACK TO THE MOUNTAINS

Two days later the Company air assaulted back into the mountainous terrain north of the Denver Trail with the 2nd Platoon in the lead. The LZ was named Harvard (BR 705720) which we quickly secured and established a defensive perimeter. Charlie Company was lifted into the same LZ. We then conducted patrols and ambushes from this area for several days with negative results. B Company then air assaulted into LZ Joe (BR 672683) where Plummer then issued orders to each of the platoons. My platoon was to conduct a patrol to the west of the LZ, find a suitable location and establish a night ambush position. Another platoon would do the same to the east of the LZ and the rest of the Company would remain on the LZ to secure the perimeter and to reinforce the two platoons, if necessary. After issuing rations the platoon moved down a ridge to a stream where we found a heavily used trail network. While evaluating the situation my point squad security spotted two armed enemy combatants moving down a trail towards us from the west. At the same instant they saw us, turned and fled back up the trail, vanishing before the point squad could initiate action against them. I made a decision to move along the same trail find a suitable ambush location and set up for the night. I felt that given the heavy use of the trail it was our best bet to spring an ambush should other enemy troops decide to use the trail. The trail angled up and away from the stream along the side of a ridge. After moving some 300-400 meters along the trail I came to the conclusion there were no really suitable sites we could occupy as the terrain to the north of the trail was too steep for us to set up positions and it would be impossible to find a rally point if we needed it. The same problem existed on the other side of the trail as it dropped off quickly to a valley below, totally unsuited for ambush positions.

After consulting with Platoon Sergeant Johnson and the squad leaders we decided to turn the platoon around and go back to the trail junction and set our ambush overlooking all the trails since the terrain around the stream gave us plenty of cover as well as an escape route back to the Company location should the need arise. I was uneasy doing this since we had been spotted earlier at the trail junction, but also knew there was no other suitable location along the route we had traversed, and nightfall was fast descending on us. The CP was notified of our intention and expressed no opposition. We then headed back to the stream. The going was rough and slow, but I wanted to move back as cautiously and quietly as possible, in the event the stream crossing was under surveillance. We arrived without incident as dusk was turning to night. I established where I wanted the machine guns set up. One covering the trail that ran along the stream and the other covering the trail going westward into the mountains. The ambush was a line ambush general following the stream from north to south. Claymores mines were placed at the junction of the trails. I told everyone to dig at least prone firing positions since we had been spotted earlier and there was a possibility the enemy may return with additional forces. I and my command group then dug in near the center of our line about 20 yards from the stream junction. By this time it was almost totally dark and I estimated we were located some 400 meters west and below the company's night defensive position (NDP). The platoon was amazingly quiet as they prepared their three man positions. I notified the company CP when we were in position and ready should any enemy force try to move along either of the trails or the stream bed. I was still concerned that some of the men had failed to dig in properly, but it was too late and dark to check their positions. It was now basically a wait and see situation and it didn't take long.

Around 1100 hours an artillery round screamed over our position and exploded about 25 meters behind our positions, followed shortly by three more rounds. Dirt and debris showered down on us. Believing the company was calling in H&I fires I broke radio silence and called for an immediate cease fire as the rounds were impacting too close for comfort. Their reply "we have not called for any artillery fire" was chilling to say the least. Needless to say those of the platoon who had failed to dig in as told were now digging furiously with anything they could get their hands on including steel pots. Several more rounds screamed over us, but this time impacted much closer to the company NDP. Plummer radioed Battalion and found that no US or ARVN artillery units had fired any rounds in our sector. Battalion also said no friendly artillery units were located in the suspected area where the firing had come from. They in turn called for and placed artillery on the suspected firing positions. In the meantime, now expecting a possible ground attack, I placed the platoon on 100% alert. Nothing more happened. Early the next morning we returned to the company perimeter to find several poncho shelters had been shredded by shrapnel, but no one was injured. The Company also had been notified by Battalion that several days previous the Division had received intelligence that an enemy force with elephants carrying artillery pieces had been sighted in the mountains to our west, but had given little or no credence to the reporting. So much for getting the word out to the troops on the ground.

As Operation Crazy Horse wound down the company patrolled further to the west over the course of the next two days. While on point for the company the platoon came across several Viet Cong laying out a punji stake field. Punji stakes were normally made of sharpened bamboo and were dipped in feces or other matter to inflict serious infections in the wound. They fled to the south and giving chase with several troopers I ended up receiving a minor punji stake wound in my left leg while trying to avoid a stake that had been mounted on a tree at throat level. Though taking the VC squad under fire, none were apparently hit and they managed to escape, easy to do in the triple canopy jungle. My leg wound was treated by SP5 "Doc" Arrellano, the senior medic and since the Company would be out of the mountains the next morning he did not call for a MEDEVAC, nor did I want him to. By the next morning the wound had started to fester, but we had already begun our movement out of the mountains and I let it be known I would report for medical treatment once we arrived back in Base Camp.

Later that morning, while descending to the Vinh Thanh Valley down a steep trail, Lt Bill Hughes slipped and then slid about 15 meters down the steep trail only to end up at the mouth of a small cave containing several Vietnamese families. They were as surprised as he. Assuming them to be VC or at least sympathizers he took them prisoner and they accompanied us until we reached the valley floor where they were picked up by helicopter and turned over to local government control at LZ Savoy. The date was June 5, 1966 and we were soon met and moved by motor convoy back to the base camp at An Khe. Our two week plus involvement in Operation Crazy Horse had finally come to an end.

CHAPTER 17

BASE CAMP AND STAND DOWN

On returning to Camp Radcliffe we were met at the Company area by Lieutenant Colonel Levin Broughton, the Battalion Commander who commended us on a job well done and expressed his deep sorrow for the men we lost. He added steaks and beer would be served after we cleaned ourselves and our gear. We needed it after tromping through jungle and mountains for the past fifteen days, surviving on C rations. Broughton also stated we were on a complete stand down and would not be sent on any missions for several days while we recouped from this difficult operation through almost impossible terrain. The troops were then dismissed and told steaks would be ready in about an hour. The Platoon Leaders and Platoon Sergeants headed to the Platoon Sergeants tent where we shared a bottle of Wild Turkey that PSG Robinson had stored for just such an occasion. It was finished post haste and then we all retired to clean ourselves and equipment and then enjoy steaks and beer. I did report to the dispensary where the Battalion Surgeon cleaned and sutured my small wound and gave me a tetanus shot.

Later that evening several of the officers went to the "O" Club to have additional drinks and play poker since we were on stand down and would not be assigned any missions for at least a couple of days. Wishful thinking. About the time we sat down with drinks and cards a barrage of incoming explosions resonated from the direction of the Division

And the Tears Flowed

helipad, better known as the Golf Course. There was no question that the base camp was being mortared. So much for a relaxing evening. Every officer in the bar immediately headed back to their respective company areas under complete blackout conditions to find out what the hell was going on. We were instructed to round up our men who had also been taking part in libations at their respective clubs or had retired for the night. Needless to say it was bedlam. Officers and NCOs alike were frantically attempting to make sense of the chaos. After about ten minutes partial order was restored and we were instructed by Plummer to form our platoons and move to our predesignated defensive positions and prepare for a possible ground attack on the base camp. As soon as we started moving the order was rescinded and we were told to move instead to the Mustang helipad and prepare for an air assault to an as yet undetermined location. The command group and the 3rd Platoon were to lead the assault.

No sooner had we organized for pickup at the Mustang Pad, the order was changed again and we were told to proceed on foot to the Golf Course helipad for pickup. I'm thinking to myself "what the hell." Of the platoon members I could find half, were still shit faced drunk, had not slept for over 24 hours, and yet the higher ups expected us to move over half a mile in complete darkness and prepare for an air assault to an as yet undetermined location. Have these idiots lost their minds." Not to mention that during the move, several of the troopers fell out vomiting or simply they were in no condition to make the trek. Hell, I didn't even have my normal RTO, Bob Mullins. He couldn't be found in the ensuing confusion so I ordered one of the men to grab the PRC 25 radio and he became my RTO. I had no idea whether or not he even knew how to use it, but told him he would learn fast. I still don't remember who it was I selected. I found out later Mullins had indulged in a little to much and had went to sleep under his cot.

On arrival at the Golf Course I estimated I only had about two thirds of my platoon. The remainder had either not been found in the confusion or had fallen out on the march to the helipad. I also noted that two rows of helicopters were already lined up along the runway and waiting for the upcoming assaults. We received word to mount up from Captain Plummer, but still had no idea where we were going. Myself and the squad leader complied by loading each of the choppers with six men per ship. Charlie Company was doing the same thing on the other line of choppers. Plummer then called all platoon leaders and platoon sergeants to the front of the column of choppers so he could brief us on the mission. We were to be inserted on an LZ several kilometers northwest of the base camp and would sweep back toward the green line attempting to find the mortar location or the enemy force that had conducted the attack. Bravo would hit their LZ first and Charlie Company would follow closely after us and conduct a similar assault into an LZ about a kilometer to our south and would simultaneously sweep back to the base perimeter with the same mission, find the enemy and mortars if possible.

Just as Plummer concluded the briefing the lift ships took off as we watched in total surprise. The CO immediately started screaming into the radio to bring the choppers back, there were no leaders on any of the ships. Myself, and the others thought "oh shit with no illumination the troops we had so patiently placed on the ships are going to jump off thinking they had reached the target LZ and in all likelihood are going to jump off and start firing." Thankfully the latter didn't happen. About five minutes later the ships returned and landed where they had previously been. Sure enough the troopers jumped from the ships, but they did not open fire as was normal in an air assault; however, they did scramble away for the ships to secure a perimeter. Both companies platoon leaders and platoon sergeants were screaming at the troops to halt and return to the choppers. Finally with much cajoling all were remounted into the choppers and with the officers and NCOs now aboard the air assault resumed. The 2nd platoon and the Command Group were now on first lift.

As we approached the assigned LZ, I could see the artillery preparation on an opening in the jungle followed closely by gunships prepping the edges of the LZ when the artillery shifted their fires. The assault went without opposition and my squad leaders began quickly moving the troops into defensive positions as we waited for the remainder of the Company to arrive. About that time I heard a rather loud voice in the complete silence of the LZ shouting "Charlie Company form on me." I carefully made my way toward the center of the LZ where I found Captain Mozey, Charlie Company Commander and his Command Group. I told him there must be a real screw up because he was on the LZ that contained Bravo Company. With a rather loud "Shit" he immediately called for a helicopter to pick he and his group up, and take them to the correct LZ. Later I found out this was accomplished and he was delivered to his assigned LZ. We also heard that just as they landed on their assigned LZ and the ship pulled away, artillery and gunships began prepping the landing zone and surrounding area followed by an air assault by his company. Luckily no damage was done and no one injured, although I am sure it scared the hell out of those on the ground.

In the meantime the remainder of our Company had joined us on our LZ. While this was happening I took a head count and found that I had at least four of five Charlie Company soldiers mixed in with my platoon. Since they were already there Plummer told them he would notify Charlie Company they were with us and they would stay until we made it back to the Battalion Area.

Around 0200 we pushed out from the LZ with my platoon as point and began our search for the mortars. It was pitch black and to me it sounded like a herd of elephants as we bumbled through the thick underbrush, at times hacking with machetes to clear a trail. Somehow or another we found the probable mortar firing position, but no sign of mortars or the enemy. One of the other platoons then took point and around 0600, after blundering around in the jungle we finally closed on the Green Line, the perimeter of the Base Camp. Lieutenant Colonel Broughton met us as we came through the wire and then with an "I'm sorry, but Division does not believe you conducted a thorough enough search. They want you to go back out do a more complete search." Even

Plummer was astonished that they had ordered this since we had found the probable firing site. By then we had no sleep for almost 48 hours, were in some cases still hung over, and were pretty much exhausted from chopping our way through the jungle all night. He argued in vain. We were ordered to go back out. Turning around we headed back into the jungle surrounding the base camp. After we had moved some 500 meters from the wire Plummer halted the search, called the platoon leaders to his position, and told us to establish platoon perimeters and then take turns sleeping over the next four hours. He then proceeded to call in situation reports at short intervals of our supposed search. After some much needed sleep he then recalled the platoons to his location and moved us back to the Green Line where we were transported back to the Company area for a much needed rest over the next several days.

While in base camp the Battalion held a moving memorial service at the newly built Battalion Chapel for the men who had died on May 21st. It was a moving ceremony with steel helmets on inverted rifles in combat boots representing each of the men who had lost their lives during the battle. Chaplain Ralph Spears conducted the service with most of the Battalion in attendance. These men were hardened combat warriors but there were few dry eyes among those in attendance at the service.

CHAPTER 18

KONTUM, RVN

On June 10th the Company was ordered to conduct a motor march from Camp Radcliffe to the city of Kontum, a small city as I recall, about 40 kilometers north of Pleiku and not far from the Cambodian/Laotian border. The movement would take most of the day. Around 0900 hours the 2 1/2 ton trucks arrived at the battalion area and we proceeded to load up and begin our journey. I was wondering why in the hell were we going by road when the Division had more helicopters than any other unit in Vietnam, but no explanation was ever forthcoming. I assumed most were probably involved in supporting one of the other Brigades of the Division. Usually two of the Brigades were involved in operations somewhere in II Corps, while the third pulled security duty at Camp Radcliffe or Highway 19 security. We departed Camp Radcliffe and headed west on QL19 the main route from Qui Nhon on the coast through the city of Pleiku and then to the border with Cambodia. Soon we were climbing out of the An Khe Valley and through the Mang Yang Pass. Needless to say everyone was on high alert while we drove slowly up and through the pass on the steep winding road to the summit, with heavy elephant grass on both sides of the highway intermingled with patches of heavy jungle, and then started down toward the Pleiku Plateau and the city of Pleiku itself. On reaching the town we passed Camp Holloway, the scene of a major NVA attack in early 1965 and one of the major catalysts for introducing US main force units into Vietnam. We then turned north towards Kontum.

The trip went without incident much to our relief and we were soon pulling perimeter duty at the airfield just to the north of town.

Duty for the most part in Kontum was fairly easy. There was a river to the east of town where we could take our troops and allow them to swim, wash the grime from their clothes, and bathe. Of course bare breasted Montagnard women used the same river to wash their clothes to the delight of the men. Kontum had a high ethnic population of hill tribesmen, mainly Jarai, Bahnar, Sedang as well as a few others, most friendly to U.S. troops.

Each evening Captain Plummer would hold meetings with the platoon leaders and lay out the next day's schedule; which platoons would go out on patrol, who would conduct training, etc. It was during these company meetings I began to notice what I felt was rising tension between Plummer and Lt. Heath even though Heath had only been with the Company for less than a month. Heath tended to question almost everything Plummer said, especially if it concerned his platoon, so much so that on several occasions Plummer even uttered the phrase "that is a direct order Lieutenant." I felt that sooner or later open hostilities between the two was going to occur. When not on patrol Plummer expected the platoon leaders and NCOs to conduct training classes with their troops such as first aid, map reading, and hand-to-hand combat to keep their combat skills sharp. I was conducting such a class on hand-to-hand combat with my platoon when LtCol Broughton, the Battalion Commander drove up in a jeep and observed the training. While taking a break he called me over and said "Mac, you don't look well. I want you to report to the Aid Station and see the Battalion Surgeon." I told him I was a little tired, but otherwise felt fine. He reiterated "I want you to see the Doc." I said I would, then resumed training as he drove off. I did not follow his instructions.

The next morning around 0800 hours the Colonel again pulled up in the platoon area and this time ordered me into the jeep where he proceeded to chew my butt for not obeying his instructions to see the doctor the previous da. I insisted I was fine and he in turn ignored me and drove me to the aid station where I was examined. The doctor said my temperature and other vitals appeared normal but he was going to keep me overnight for observation.

The next morning, although I kept insisting nothing was wrong, he drove me to the 15th Med Aid Station for blood work and further observation. On arrival a medic took my vitals and drew blood. About a dozen or so other troopers were in the tent with me. About 30 minutes later the Corpsman returned and said to the waiting crowd "Only one of you has malaria and I bet I can point him out", turning he looked at me and said "Lieutenant, come with me." In the meantime, during the wait I had developed a headache and was suddenly feeling feverish. I was escorted to another tent containing several cots and was told to undress and lay down. Another medic then took my temperature and additional blood. By then my fever had soared dramatically to 103 degrees. The first medic was then joined by several others and they began rubbing me down with alcohol to reduce the fever, then when that didn't work, poured buckets of ice over me. I do not remember much other than chills followed by a rampaging fever. I now knew I was one sick puppy.

CHAPTER 19

EVACUATION TO CAMP ZAMA, JAPAN

The next thing I do remember was being placed on a C130 aircraft and being flown to the 85th Evacuation Hospital in Qui Nhon. On arrival I was assigned to a ward with about 20 other patients. My temperature varied reaching as high of 104 degrees. Again, ice and alcohol rubs were used to bring it under control. I was burning up one minute and freezing the next. I do remember the nurses trying to comfort me. I also remember they kept saying I was a very sick individual and once they stabilized me I would be transferred to a hospital in Japan. All I know is these Angels of Mercy were with me almost constantly while I was at the 85th Evac Hospital. After a week I was finally placed on a stretcher and loaded on an U.S. Air Force Aircraft along with other ill and wounded men. The stretchers were placed in such a manner that they reached from the floor to the roof of the aircraft with very little room between stretchers, maybe a foot apart. The plane was full \and we were well taken care of by Air Force nurses who served aboard the aircraft.

We flew to Clark Field in the Philippines then, I believe, to Tachikawa Air Force Base just to west of Central Tokyo where we were then transported by hospital buses to Camp Zama Army Hospital south of Tokyo. I was placed in a ward with several other officers. The next few days were a blur as I went from wakefulness to hours of sleeping until the fever finally abated. Japanese nurses and assistants tended us under the supervision of U.S. Army nurses. After finally gaining control of my senses I met the other guys on the ward, even though I only remember a couple, 1st Lt Jim Murray and 1st Lt David Hadley. Jim was also from the 1st Cav, the 1/12th Cavalry and David was a former Officer Candidate classmate of mine who had been wounded while serving with the 101st Airborne near Tuy Hoa. Jim and I became fast friends and spent a lot of time together in Japan. I do recall one other on the ward was an Australian who was commissioned as a Lieutenant in the U.S. Army and was also serving with the 101st Airborne when wounded near Tuy Hoa while serving under the leadership of Lieutenant Colonel David Hackworth, his Battalion Commander. Hackworth was a highly decorated Lieutenant Colonel who served in both WWII and Korea, but the Aussie did not have kind words for him. He said his unit was in heavy contact with a VC Main Force unit when they attempted to cross an open rice paddy. Hackworth again and again kept sending troops into the paddy, resulting in numerous friendly killed or wounded, before the enemy withdrew.

I was soon examined by Dr. (Major) William Reed who told me I had Plasmodium Falciparum malaria, a type of malaria that can be deadly if not treated promptly. He said they had done a good job in Vietnam in starting treatment and that I was being treated with quinine and I should recover completely. He said I was also being treated for Salmonella (food poisoning) and had intestinal worms. Treatment for this would take place the next day. Sure enough a cute Japanese nurse's assistant came to the ward, smiled, handed me a capsule about the size of a walnut, and told me to go to the latrine and take the pill when I got there. I asked why the latrine to take a pill. She smiled and said in broken English "as soon as you take it sit on the benjo (commode)." I did as told and headed for the latrine. I gagged as I took the horse pill she had given me. It tasted like I imagined kerosene would taste and left a horrible lingering taste in my mouth and throat. I did everything I could not to throw up and headed for the toilet. Within minutes I began to severely cramp and then was hit with an explosion of diarrhea like never before. It felt like I was on the commode forever with numerous bowel movements and there was no question I was completely empty when I finally was able to leave the bathroom weak and exhausted. I drug myself back to my bed and lay there the rest of the day scared to move lest I crap all over myself. Around suppertime I finally began feeling normal and was ready to eat again.

Every morning my blood was drawn and tested to monitor the progress of treatment for the malaria. After a week Dr. Reed said the treatment was working and I would be released from the hospital to the Bachelor Officer Housing at Camp Zama, but would have to report daily to the hospital for continued observation and testing. This was great news to me. I asked how long this would go on and he said at least 30 more days then I would be returned to Vietnam. I asked if there were any restrictions on anything. He said no, just what we had discussed. The next day I moved from the hospital into the BOQ.

While in the hospital Jim Murray and I had made friends with the American head nurse on the ward. She was a Major, whose name I cannot recall, and asked if we would like to see a little of the countryside now that we were no longer restricted to the hospital. Off course we quickly agreed. She had a car and we would spend the day off with her as she drove.

We left early the next morning and drove southwest toward the quaint town of Hakone. We soon realized just how beautiful the Japanese countryside was. We could see Mount Fujiyama off to the Southwest and it was a sight to see as it towered over all the other mountains in the area. We were soon driving along the Pacific Ocean with beautiful beaches and some rugged shoreline. About an hour later we reached the town of Hakone, which is considered a resort area by the Japanese. We soon found out why. The town was spotless with beautiful gardens and architecture. Lake Hakone (also known as Lake Ashinoko) was one of the most beautiful lakes Jim and I had ever seen. Crystal blue and clear water sparkling below the towering height of Mount Fuji in the distance. Flowers were in abundance as were temples throughout the area. We drove completely around the lake, one of the largest in the area, finally stopping for lunch at a small restaurant overlooking the lake. The view was spectacular and the food ample and delicious. As I recall we all had a tempura shrimp dish with accompanying vegetables and sauces. All in all a great day, but more was to come. That evening the Major drove us into Tokyo and the Ginza area of the city where we then enjoyed a great dinner at a Mongolian Barbeque restaurant. You selected what you wanted from a table full of meats, seafood, and vegetables and the chef then prepared the meal on a grill on the table in front of you. Again, simply delicious cuisine with Kirin beer aplenty. Following the meal we then enjoyed some of the Japanese night life at several night clubs and bars that were in abundance in the Ginza area. Late that night we returned to Camp Zama and retired for the night. All in all a simply glorious day.

The next day Jim and I decided to go to Yokuska, a navy town on Tokyo Bay about 45 minutes by train from Zama station. The trip went fast and we were soon amid the bustle of a typical Japanese city. The first stop was at a Navy Club Mess, where we enjoyed a great breakfast. The Navy sure knew how to live and after we scarfed down eggs, steak, fresh fruit, coffee, etc., we headed out to find a steam bath and massage parlor. We were greeted warmly and told the matron at the desk we wanted the works she escorted us to the rear where we were greeted by several scantily clad young ladies who proceeded to lead us to a steam room with steam cabinets. After undressing and being handed a small towel we were each placed in cabinets where the steam was turned up so high it actually became almost unbearable. Following the bath we were shown into a shower area where the ladies then bathed us before rinsing us of and leading us to what appeared to be a large swimming pool. Entering the water we found it was heated and delightful. The coup de grace however; was the massage that followed. For almost an hour the young ladies pounded, and kneaded every part of our bodies.

When done we could barely walk back to the dressing room. All this for $3.00. We were in heaven and hated to depart.

Back on the streets we did some sightseeing and then stopped to have lunch, before heading back to the BOQ. I had Sukiyaki, a mixture of beef and vegetables, while Jim opted for sashimi, a dish of raw thinly sliced fish. He picked his own fish from a tank located in the center of the restaurant. The waitress looked at him like he was crazy since he chose an eel, but she netted the fish he pointed at and took it off to be prepared. Soon we were enjoying our meals and both our selections were surprisingly good. I knew mine would be since I had sukiyaki several times before when I was stationed at Fort Ord. With stops at several bars in the area we soon caught the train and headed back to Camp Zama.

CHAPTER 20

ZAMA – AND A GIRL NAMED MIYOKA

While in the hospital I had talked to Dave Hadley just after he had received orders returning him to duty. He told me about a little club not too far from Camp Zama and said I should check it out once I got settled into the BOQ. He said it was a short taxi ride and I should ask for Michiko if I went there. Hadley had spent time with her and said she was a knockout and a great lady to get to know. Of course, taking his suggestion to heart, that evening I hailed a taxi and made my way to the bar. I noticed several other bars also grouped around this bar. Never having been in a bar in Zama City I really did not know what to expect, but I knew they probably all catered to U.S. servicemen since Camp Zama and Atsugi Naval Air Station were both located within five miles of the town of Zama and I had seen other Americans on the streets as we drove there.

Entering the bar Hadley had mentioned, I was greeted by an older, but attractive woman, who welcomed me to her bar speaking perfect English. She escorted me to a booth and said a waitress would be with me in a moment. As she walked away a young lady approached, said hello, and asked what I would like to drink in almost perfect English. I asked if her name was Michiko, since Dave had really given me no definitive description other than she was pretty, and this young lady was certainly cute. She responded saying I'm sorry, but it is Michiko's night off. I must have looked a little disappointed; however, she just smiled and said "maybe you come tomorrow night when Michiko is working." I said "no that's okay I'm here now" and then asked her name. She smiled and said "my name is Miyoko." "Okay, Miyoko I will take a beer." She responded "we only have Kirin or Sapporo no American." I chose the Kirin, only because I had heard the name previously while stationed in California.

When she returned with the beer it was the size of a a quart bottle, was ice cold and tasted really good. I asked her how much and it was something like $.25, which I could not believe for a beer that size. I knew right then I was going to like this place. I asked Miyoko if she was allowed to sit with customers and she said yes, not a problem. I kind of figured this was probably going to be her answer since there was only one other customer, the owner, and another waitress in the bar at the time. We chatted with her asking if I was stationed at Atsugi or Zama. I told her I was actually stationed in Vietnam, but had been in the hospital at Zama. She asked me how long before I had to return to Vietnam and I told her it would probably be sometime in late July or early August. After a couple beers and small chatter I told her I better head back to Zama. She then told me the bar closed at 11:00 p.m. since the area was patrolled by the Navy out of Atsugi, NAS; however, there was a nightclub a couple of miles away that remained open until 2:00 a.m., since it was under control of the Army out of Camp Zama. She said the club had a dance floor and a live band. It didn't take long for me to decide I needed to check this out and, of course, I asked Miyoko if she would like to show me where the club was located. She smiled and said okay.

At 11:00 we headed for the new club. There was no cover charge as I recall and we were escorted to a table near the dance floor. After ordering drinks we took our turn on the dance floor. Surprisingly she was an excellent dancer and the band played all the popular songs of the day. We were enjoying ourselves immensely and time seemed to fly by. Around 1:30 Miyoko suggested we go to her house, which was nearby. I was surprised by the offer and even more surprised she had her own home. I expected she would ask for money and told her I did not have very much cash. She retorted somewhat angrily she did not want money. She said she liked my company and had enjoyed being with me for the evening. Somewhat chagrined I apologized for insinuating she was a prostitute. She accepted my apology and we left the club, caught a cab, and headed to her house which was a little more than a mile away.

When we arrived I was even more surprised. The house was small but beautifully furnished and had its own bathroom with a shower and a large bedroom. She also pointed out that the owner of the bar lived right behind her. As expected I ended up spending the night and what a night it was. Here I had only met this lovely young woman and now we were making love. I could not have asked for a more beautiful evening knowing in the back of my mind a few weeks ago I did not know if I would live or die. Sadly all good things must come to an end and I told her I had to go back to the hospital and have bloodwork done. Surprisingly she asked if I would come back that night. With an invite like that all I could say was, "of course I will be back. I will meet you at your club." She said "you know Michiko will be there and that's who you really came to meet." My response, "Miyoko I don't think you have anything to worry about after the night we just spent together." She smiled shyly and said "I am so glad to hear that", kissed me and said "I look forward to seeing you tonight."

After taking a taxi to the hospital and having the required blood work done I headed to the BOQ to get some much needed sleep. Wakening around 1400 hours I headed to Finance to find out how much, if any, pay I could collect. They advanced me a couple of hundred and I then headed to the Post Exchange to buy some clothes, toiletries, and a haircut. Around 1700 hours I headed to the Officers Club and had a delicious steak dinner. Around 1900 I again hailed a taxi and headed back to the bar in the town of Zama.

Again, as I walked in the door I was greeted by the owner. Miyoko came over, bowed in the Japanese tradition then seated me in the same booth as the night before. She left to fetch me a beer and then came back with one of the most beautiful Japanese ladies I had ever laid eyes on introducing me to no other that Michiko. She also spoke very good English and said she was glad to meet me and then asked if I knew where Dave was she hadn't seen him in several days. I broke the news to her that Dave was on his way back to Vietnam. She looked a little downtrodden mentioning that Dave had made no mention that he was leaving. She left and I smiled and began talking with Miyoko. The owner came over and sat down. She asked if I would take her to the Officers Club at Camp Zama so she could play the slot machines. She said if I would she would buy both Miyoko and I dinner in return although I told her that was not necessary. I said I saw no problem with taking her which thrilled her to no end and told her just to let me know what night she wanted to go. She agreed and picked Thursday night. When Miyoko and I got ready to leave that night I asked how much my bar bill was and the response was there is no charge. The owner was letting me drink for free for taking her to the "O" Club. I thought it was only for the night, but later found I was to drink free as long as I was at her club. Needless to say I took the owner to Camp Zama on a number of occasions and let her play the slots. I need to make it clear the free drinks usually consisted of two quart size Kirin beers about all I could handle while in the bar.

Miyoko and I went to the night club and a Korean restaurant at least two nights a week before returning to her house. At the restaurant we usually had Bulgogi or Kalbi, traditional Korean cuisine, cooked on a small grill in the table in front of us. At other times we just left the bar, went to the restaurant, and then headed to her house to chat and to make love. I sometimes wondered how I survived. On one occasion at the night club I met and made friends with an Army Sergeant Major from Camp Zama who invited me to breakfast at the NCO Club. Even though I told him I was an officer and not allowed in their club he just laughed and said "Lieutenant, it's my club and you can go if I invite you." We met the next morning, a Sunday, and I had an excellent meal of steak and eggs. He enjoyed a martini filled to the top with olives. He said "I hate martinis, but loved olives." Of course no one said anything about me being there. He invited me to join him again, but feeling somewhat out of place I declined. We did run into him at the club several times over the next few weeks and I thoroughly enjoyed his company.

There were also nights that I did not go to the bar, but opted for the Zama Officers Club instead. On one of these occasions I was surprised to find Patti Paige would be performing unannounced at the club. Without a doubt one of the best shows I have ever attended. She sang for over an hour, then walked around the club greeting and hugging the patrons, many of them patients from the hospital. She then again took to the stage and performed for another hour before departing. What a lovely lady and what a great night for all in attendance.

CHAPTER 21

FAREWELL, BACK INTO THE BREECH, AND NATHAN HALE

Alas all good things must come to an end and I was notified when I went in for a checkup that I had been cleared by the doctor and would be reassigned back to my unit in Vietnam within the next several days. The orders soon came down and I was told to report on August 3rd for a flight back to Vietnam. I went to the bar that night and said my farewell to Mama San and the rest of the girls in the bar. Miyoko and I then left and went to her house to say our private farewell. She was upset, but I told her I would see her again. She did not think so, but I knew I had an R&R coming later in the year and I was determined to come back to Tokyo and spend time with Miyoko. There was not much sleep for either of us that night, but lots of tears by her, especially when I said my farewell as I headed back to base.

The next day all those returning to Vietnam were processed through the Camp Zama Personnel Center, given orders and then taken to Yokota Air Force Base for our flight back to Vietnam. Needless to say we were not real happy, but knew we still had a duty to fill. The aircraft was a civilian commercial jet, but I don't remember what airline. We departed and flew to Taiwan, where we refueled for our final leg back to Tan Son Nhut. About an hour after takeoff there was a hell of a loud bang and the aircraft immediately went nose down toward the Pacific scaring the

And the Tears Flowed

hell out of everyone, especially when the stewardess nearest me started screaming. We didn't know what had happened and all I could think was we're going into the Pacific and I doubted anyone would survive. After what seemed an eternity of rapid descent the plane began to level off. The pilot came on the intercom and told us what happened. Apparently, the seal on the back door of the aircraft had blown out and the pilot knew he would lose cabin pressure unless he descended rapidly to 10,000 feet. We had been flying at just over 30,000 feet. He also told us if we looked out the windows we would see he was dumping fuel and we would be returning to Taiwan for repairs and refueling before we again proceeded to Vietnam. Everyone on the plane let out a collective sigh of relief. After repairs and refueling we resumed our trip without incident. Shortly thereafter we were back in the "Nam".

The next day, August 8, 1966 I was a passenger on a C-130 on my way back to Camp Radcliffe and the 1st Cav Division. On arrival I was met and transported by jeep to Battalion Headquarters where I was greeted for the second time by Lieutenant Colonel Broughton. He warmly welcomed me back and after asking how I felt told me he would like me to take over the Battalion Recon Platoon. Even though I knew this to be a plum assignment I responded by telling him although I was honored he had such high regard for me, I really wanted to go back to Bravo Company and my platoon. He smiled and said he figured that would be my response, but I would not be sent back to command a platoon, Captain Plummer wanted me as his Executive Officer and had held the slot open for my return. Since that was Plummer's wish he would honor it and send me back to the best company in the battalion. He also said you know most of the men who were here with you have completed their tour of duty and the men you will be dealing with for the most part are all new, including the officers. He also said there would be a battalion formation at 0900 hours the following day for a Change of Command Ceremony. He was transferring command to a new battalion commander and that during the ceremony I was to receive a medal.

I proceeded to the company area where I was greeted by 1st Sergeant Ray Poynter, who was one of the few men still with the company, but was scheduled to leave in a few days. Again I was warmly greeted in the orderly room. Top Poynter told me his replacement was 1st Sergeant Robert Craig, who would report in a few days.

Fig 24. 1st SGT Robert Craig

Ray told me my gear was in the Company Commander's hooch, since I was now the X.O. He also said the Company had all new Lieutenants; Hughes, East, Heath, and Langston had all left. I asked why Heath, he had only arrived in May. Top said Plummer and Heath had a heated exchange in late June and Plummer had relieved him of command. I never knew the exact story, but later I asked Plummer and all he said was he relieved him for insubordination. The new lieutenants: were 2nd Lt John Riffle, 2nd Lt Tom Frye, 1st Lt Lamont Finch, and 1st Lt Ralph (Dusty) Hallenbeck. Riffle and Frye were ROTC graduates, Finch an OCS grad and Lt Hallenbeck a West Pointer. He was only with the company for a short two months before being selected to become the Aide-de-Camp to one of the Assistant Division Commanders. He was replaced by 1Lt Daniel Hennessy who assumed command of the 1st Platoon. While with the Company, Dusty performed admirably and was well liked by his troops.

I also found out from Top that the same day I was medically transferred to Qui Nhon the Company was alerted and then moved by C-130s to Tuy Hoa, the Capitol of Phu Yen Province and Operation Nathan Hale. The 101st Airborne Division was heavily engaged with Viet Cong Main Force Units and the 3rd Brigade of the 1st Cav been committed and took over the operation. Our company was placed under the operational control of its Commander, Colonel Hal Moore of LZ X-Ray fame. Moore at that time was a Lieutenant Colonel and commanded the 1st Battalion 7th Cavalry Regiment who flew into LZ X-Ray and who, for three long days and nights, fought of two NVA Regiments, who were determined to kill all the America Soldiers on the LZ. They failed in their efforts.

Even though it was early evening when the company arrived they were immediately committed. I do not recall exactly or what sequence of events transpired since I was not there, but I do know the company went into at least two hot LZs, Cherry and Apple, during the operation. While air assaulting into LZ Apple on June 24, 1966, one of the Huey's was shot down. All aboard were killed in the flaming crash including SSGT Bobby James, the Platoon Sergeant of the 3rd platoon, Sp4 Johnnie Hickey, and my former medic Sp4 Adell Alston.

Fig 25. SSGT Bobby James   Fig 26. SP4 Johnny Hickey

The following day SSG Charles Edwards was also killed while assaulting into one of the hot LZs. All were truly outstanding soldiers.

Fig 27. SSGT Charles Edwards

I also learned that several days later on Bravo Company was sent to the aid of a company of the 101st who had been heavily mauled by a VC Main Force unit. They were located on a tabletop mountain named position Eagle and when our company arrived at dusk they were able to slip in, apparently unnoticed, by the enemy battalion. The company found the 101st troopers in bad shape from having to withstand numerous assaults and mortar attacks on their position, and many had sustained wounds. They were also short of ammunition, water and rations. Plummer secured the perimeter, again apparently unnoticed by the VC Main Force unit. He held one platoon, Lt Heath's, as a reaction force in reserve near the company CP. He also ordered the platoon leaders to have their men on 50% alert during the night and to be prepared to fire a "mad minute" at 0500 hours. A "mad minute" meant all small arms, except the machine guns, would fire a full magazine to catch the enemy off guard if they were preparing to attack. It worked like a charm. Just as the company opened fire the VC unit stood up to charge the position they though was still occupied by a lone company of soldiers they had almost decimated the day before, but instead ran right into a firestorm of bullets from the two companies now occupying the table top mountain. It was devastating to the enemy main force battalion, with a significant number of enemy combatants killed as they charged the perimeter, 134 in all. They quickly evacuated the battle area after sustaining a staggering defeat at the hands of Bravo Company, who suffered not a single casualty during the battle. Plummer was awarded the Silver Star Medal later that day by MG Stanley Larsen who flew in to congratulate the Company on their stunning victory. This victory also brought to a close the Company's participation in Nathan Hale.

Fig 28. MG Stanley Larsen

The Company was on a day operation when I reported back in, but I do not recall exactly where or what they were doing. There were the usual number of soldiers in the company area waiting DEROS (Date Estimated to Return from Overseas), returning to duty as I was, or were preparing for or coming from Rest & Recuperation (R&R). I told Top I was going to get settled into the Commanders Hooch and then check out the Company area. Believe it or not I was glad to be back and was looking forward to assuming my duties as X.O.

Once I secured my personal items I walked through the area. As I approached one of the GP Medium platoon tents at the lower end of the company area I heard voices. The tent flap was closed, which was unusual. Opening it and walking in I found four individuals engaged in a poker game, which was not allowed in the company area. One of them realizing I was there called the other to attention. I proceeded to where they were playing reached down and confiscated all the money in the pot. I thanked them for donating to the company fund, said gambling was only allowed in the EM Club, and told them to report to the orderly room where I would meet them.

As I left the tent one of the soldiers asked if he could talk to me. I told him to meet me outside. As I waited he came through the flap and I was stunned to see Charles Allen, a close friend and barber from my home town of Newport News, Virginia. Charles was a blond headed man who always had a smile on his face.

Fig 29. SP4 Charles Allen, Supply Clerk

He saluted which I returned. Charles said, "Come on Bill, you're not going to give us a shit detail are you. Hell we were friends and used to play cards all the time back home." With a smile I responded "Private Allen, its Lieutenant McCarron and we are not back home. Now you and the others get your asses up to the orderly room, report to the 1st Sergeant, and tell him I want you all put on detail." Allen's face dropped and he and the others took off as directed. Top ended up having them work as Environmental Sanitation Engineers (Shit Burning Detail) and then on beautifying the area by raking rocks and bare ground for the rest of the day.

Later that evening I sent for Charles and had him report to my hooch. He was a little hesitant when he arrived, but saluted and said he was told I wanted to see him. I smiled and welcomed him to the company, invited him to have a drink with me and informed him he would not be assigned to a platoon as a rifleman, but rather was going to be assigned as an assistant supply clerk. Not only that but he would become the company barber. He said "Lieutenant, I'm a rifleman and know nothing about supply." My response was "you'll learn, but there is no way you are going to the field as a rifleman. I've been there and I want to see you survive your year here." There was no further discussion. We enjoyed our drink and reminisced about our home town and how all our old friends were doing. It was a great conversation since I had not seen any of them for almost two years. In the meantime the company had returned to base camp.

The next morning I preceded to the parade field and reported to Col Broughton and his staff who were assembled near the Battalion Chapel. It was there I learned I was to be awarded a medal for valor during the Change of Command ceremony which was about to take place. Once the troops were lined up in formation for the ceremony we proceeded to the front of the formation. They were called to attention and Brigadier General William Becker proceeded to award Col Broughton the Legion of Merit for his leadership of the Battalion over the past five months. I was absolutely stunned when BG Becker then turned to me and awarded me the Silver Star Medal for Gallantry during the May 21st battle. I never felt I had done anything special other than command my platoon during the battle. To be awarded the third highest medal for valor that can be given by the United States Military left me speechless.

Fig 30. BG William Becker

I remember Col Broughton turning to me and saying "I would give up this Legion of Merit anytime for one of those. You earned it." The ceremony ended with Battalion Colors being passed from Broughton to our new commander, Lieutenant Colonel William Louisell who had recently arrived from duty in the Pentagon. I hated to see Broughton depart. I personally thought he had done a great job as the Battalion Commander. Other officers in the Battalion though otherwise, but would never convince me he did not. I simply was not sure about Louisell. From what I heard most of his career had been spent serving in the Pentagon. Several days later 1SGT Craig took over from Ray Poynter. Craig was a tall slender figure of a man, stern but fair, with a dry sense of humor and I immediately took a strong liking towards him.

A few days later my suspicions about Louisell proved to be right. The company was alerted to move a platoon to the Mustang Helipad for pick up in support of troops in contact. The designated platoon moved quickly to the LZ while I called the 227th Aviation Battalion to find out how the helicopters would be landing. I was told they would be in a heavy right formation, meaning three helicopters would be to the right of the lead, and two would be to the left. I immediately lined up the sticks (six men to a chopper) on each side of the helipad so they could mount quickly as soon as the helicopters landed. I noticed our new Battalion Commander was standing near the top of the helipad observing what was going on. To my dismay, the helicopters came in heavy left, three helicopters to the left as they landed and two to the right. Confusion was immediate as troops started scrambling for the nearest helicopter creating complete bedlam on the LZ. Finally the ships were loaded and the platoon was on the way to support the unit in contact. As I turned to head back to the company area Louisell shouted, "Lieutenant, report to me immediately." I did as I was told knowing an ass chewing would be forthcoming. He was almost livid when he asked, "What the hell was that." I tried to explain the Aviation Battalion had told me the helicopters would come in heavy right and based on that I had lined the troops up accordingly. He said "That is not what I am talking about. None of those men boarding the choppers fastened their seat belts or chin straps. That is totally uncalled for." I thought to myself the whole pickup was a cluster fuck and he is upset because they didn't fasten their seatbelts. I explained they couldn't fasten seat belts since the seats in the Huey's were in an upright position so the troops sat on the floor of the aircraft usually with their feet on the skids so they could rapidly disembark from the aircraft should the LZ be hot (i.e., under fire from enemy forces as they landed). He was somewhat mollified, but continued to harangue me, even though he conceded he didn't know the seats were strapped in an upright position, but there was still no excuse for the chin straps being loose. I knew I was never going to win that argument so I just kept my mouth shut. Still not finished he asked if I knew how to report to a senior officer, meaning I did not salute when I reported. I pointed out we were in a combat zone and by saluting I was placing a target on his back as a senior officer should an enemy sniper be in the area. This really was not true, we did salute in the battalion area, but it got me out of a sticky situation. When on operations in the field however, the normal procedure was not to salute and identify officers. Without another word he turned and walked back towards his headquarters. The committed platoon returned later that day to the company area without making contact. Apparently the Victor Charlies had broken contact and withdrawn as our troops arrived. The remainder of the month was a blur. I seem to recall we again pulled duty along Highway 19, as well as some defensive patrolling around the base camp, but had no contact with any enemy forces.

CHAPTER 22

OPERATION THAYER 1 AND LZ HAMMOND

In early September 1966 the 1st Cav kicked off Operation Thayer I, a two Brigade operation to the east of Ahn Ke in Binh Dinh Province which bordered the East China Sea. We were also supported on the operation by the Army of Vietnam and Korean Army forces. Binh Dinh Province had long been a major rice growing area and a stronghold of the Viet Cong/NVA and its sympathizers. Not a nice place to operate in, but the Cav was determined to deny the NVA/VC its rice supply and to win the support of the population in the province. It also allowed the Vietnamese to hold free elections without the threat of enemy interference. Our company along with the other elements of the Battalion and the remainder of the 1st Brigade were moved to LZ Hammond, which was established as the Forward Headquarters and Operating Base of the 1st Cav Division. Hammond was distinguished by a large hill dominating the center of the LZ encircled by a perimeter running around its base. The first line of defense was a tangle of concertina wire about 300 meters from the lower part of the dominant hill mass and were backed by additional fences. They were followed by fighting positions established to protect the various battalion train areas (a train area is a forward supply area to support the units in the field and also includes medical and maintenance facilities.) Each company also had its own train area located within the battalion train area and they were expected to defend their areas with their lives if need be. These positions were manned at night by both Division personnel and men of the line units from each of the battalion trains areas. Most support elements of the Division were represented on the LZ. It included an Army airfield on the east side of the hill which could handle USAF C-130s and C-123s as well as US Army Caribou aircraft. There was also a large parking area for helicopters. Major Helicopter assaults could be conducted from there anytime day or night.

Phu Cat Air Force Base was located some six kilometers to the south and was capable of providing fighter support if needed. The port city of Qui Nhon was about 30 kilometers further south from there. Hammond was to remain the Forward Operating Base for the remainder of the year. In late January 1967 it was moved to LZ English just north of the town of Bong Son. Also, in September, we were informed the Army had removed the Brigades designation as an "Airborne" unit. They had determined that the use of parachutes was next to impossible in the terrain in the Central Highlands of Vietnam. Like the rest of the Division we were now designated as "Airmobile". Those receiving airborne pay; however, would continue to receive jump pay until they rotated back to the States. Anyone joining the unit after the announcement, even though airborne qualified would not receive the bonus "jump pay, $55.00 for Enlisted and $110.00 for Officers." All companies of the Battalion were committed against the 18th and 22nd NVA Regiments as well as main force Viet Cong units who had used the mountains terrain in Binh Dinh Province as a base of operations and haven for years.

After establishment of the Forward Operating Base at Hammond the 1st Brigade began conducting combat operations to eliminate the PAVN (NVA) and Viet Cong (VC) forces who had long established a strong presence throughout the province and were taxing and proselytizing the population to their cause. It did not take much persuasion for the locals to turn over a large portion of their rice yield to the communist forces. The overall mission of the 1st Cav was to prevent these local/main force units forces access to the villages and hamlets within the rich rice producing areas of the province and eliminate them if possible. The LZ itself included most of the division support units (i.e., Division Support Command, 15th Med, a POW compound, Aviation units, helipads, and a runway that could handle C-130s and Caribou aircraft). These were located to the north, south and east of the hill mass. The $1/8^{th}$ was located to the west of the hill. For the most part rice paddies surrounded the LZ with tree lines several hundred yards from the perimeter that had been established. There were also several villages/hamlets about 500 to 1500 meters from the perimeter.

Within hours of arrival at LZ Hammond the companies of the 1/8 Cav air assaulted into various locations in the mountainous area of the Province known as the Crows Foot or by some as the Eagles Claw and began search and destroy operations throughout the Kim Song Valley and surrounding areas. The Battalion Headquarters area, the Tactical Operations Center and the locations of the company supply trains area of the $1/8^{th}$ were quickly established so they could provide the necessary support to the units deploying to the field. Defensive positions were dug around the perimeter of the LZ and were manned by Division support personnel and any replacement personnel reporting back for duty or leaving for RR/DEROS.

While in the supply/trains area I was assisted by Staff Sergeant Bill Odom, the acting company rear First Sergeant, and our two supply clerks, SP4 Charles Allen and PFC Tom Silensky.

Fig 31. 1st SGT Robert Craig and SSGT Bill Odom at LZ Hammond

Our first task after the company deployed was to help establish the Battalion and company areas; make sure the company in the field was adequately supplied with necessary essentials and at least one hot meal a day if the situation allowed; and to begin construction of bunkers for our own protection should the LZ be attacked. The four of us, with the help of SGT Herman Rush who was in the company train area recovering from foot problems, began by initially filling empty ammunition crates with sand and then stacked them on top of each other making an outline of a rectangular shaped bunker with firing apertures. We then filled sand bags and placed them around the ammo crates two bags deep. Sp4 Allen somehow secured some PCP metal planking and we placed that to form the roof. Three layers of sandbags on top of the PCP competed construction of the bunker. We were proud of our accomplishment and little did we know several nights later we would use it.

Meanwhile the Company was conducting search and destroy missions in the mountains overlooking the Soui Ca Valley. Sp4 Asher related they witnessed a helicopter taking fire from a small hill. His Lieutenant then ordered two squads from the platoon to accompany him to search the hill and eliminate any enemy they may encounter. As they moved up the hill the point man shot and killed one VC soldier and captured another. The platoon element then started back down the hill with Asher's fire team now in the lead. As they passed the fire team who had been on point, the lead individual warned him there were more enemy soldiers just to their front along the trail. As Asher moved forward he spotted an enemy soldier and took him under fire, killing him. The others scattered into the jungle. The one he killed turned out to be an NVA officer wearing a pistol. Another enemy combatant then reemerged from the thick underbrush and Asher was able to also kill him also. The remainder of the enemy vanished into the thick jungle. With that the platoon returned to their original position along the stream where they linked up with the rest of the Company and resumed their search and destroy mission.

On 23 September, at 0100hrs LZ Hammond came under a mortar and recoilless rifle attack by the 2nd Viet Cong Regiment of the 3rd Division. The attack lasted a little over 10 minutes and there were no ground assaults attempted. At least 11 rounds of 82mm mortars and over 40 rounds of 60mm mortars were fired at the LZ. An unknown number of recoilless rifle rounds also hit the perimeter. The attack resulted in one US KIA and 32 friendly WIA on Hammond. Seventeen aircraft were damaged, six severe enough to be evacuated for repair. When the attack started Odom, Allen, and myself were sleeping in a small GP tent next to the bunker. As soon as I heard the first mortar round hit I yelled "incoming" and we all jumped up and ran for the tent exit and the safety of the bunker. Fortunately, I stumbled over a cardboard box we were using for trash near the entrance to the tent and fell forward. Simultaneously, a 57mm round went through the tent right where I had been standing and exploded about 25 yards behind the tent. Another round exploded about 30 yards to our right in Delta Company's area wounding 1Lt. Albert Hayes, their Executive Officer, as he ran to his bunker. Al survived but unfortunately was later killed in February 1967. To my knowledge no one else in the Battalion area was injured. Counter mortar fire and artillery were fired almost immediately at suspected enemy firing locations to our Northwest as well as possible routes of withdrawal. Gunships also attacked suspected areas, including routes of egress from the area. At first light the 1/9th Cav and the Support Command conducted sweeps and found the firing positions for the mortars and the recoilless rifles. They also captured 15 VC suspects, one while he was trying to conceal an 82mm mortar round; however, the main body of the 2nd VC Regiment escaped detection and moved back to the northeast and eventually to their base in the Cay Giep Mountains.

(Note: I later found a short article in a book, "Infantry in Vietnam" by LTC Albert N. Garland which described the attack based on captured documents and POW interrogations. The attack on LZ Hammond was planned by a Major Khanh, Regimental Commander of the 2nd Viet Cong Regiment. Khanh, after a thorough recon of Hammond by guerrillas of the regiment, wanted to conduct both direct and indirect fire attacks, followed by a ground assault on the base. He was overruled by Gen Truc, the Division Commander. Gen Truc said he could not provide either the 18th Regiment or the 22nd Regiment to support a ground assault; however, he did approve the weapons attack. Of interest is that Khanh, beginning on 19 September, moved his regiment from the Cay Giep Mountain to the west then south to attack LZ Hammond, which was located some 36 miles as the crow flies, but was probably closer to 60 miles, without being detected. No doubt, he was aided immensely by local force guerrillas and sympathizers who meticulously planned the routes for his force so they could be in position to attack in the early morning hours of September 23, 1966. After the attack he withdrew his force back to the Cay Giep Mountains, again with the assistance of local guerrillas, laying booby traps along his withdrawal route. On 29 September, fearing his force was vulnerable to attack because of US troop deployments into the Cay Giep area, Khanh then moved his regiment some twenty kilometers to the west and south into the Kim Son Valley, which afforded him more running and concealment room. Again, none of the movement was detected by US or RVN forces).

[1] Infantry in Vietnam Small Unit Actions in the Early Days: 1965-66 by LTC Albert N. Garland, USA (Ret) 1967.)

In early October the company began operations further North in the Binh Dinh AO to conduct operation in mountainous areas nearer the coast. In midmonth they moved to the top of a large mountain mass separating the An Lao Valley and the Bong Son Plains in an attempt to flush and search out any enemy forces using the area as a base. No enemy troops or base camps were found and once they reached the uppermost heights they realized they had a panoramic view of the land below which stretched all the way to the South China Sea. However, all good things must come to an end. As evening descended a heavy bank of fog rolled in from the South China Sea and enveloped the entire mountain top, virtually cutting the company completely off from the outside world. For over a week the company was stranded on the mountain with dwindling food supplies and virtually no visibility. Attempt after attempt was made to get a log ship to them with supplies, but with no success. The pilots simply would not fly into the fog bank. On top of that Division was now ordering us to get Captain Plummer of the mountain. He had been promoted to Major and was scheduled to take over the Division Training Program for newly arriving troops. Captain Raul Villaronga, the S-1 was coming from An Khe and would replace him.

Fig 32. Captain Raul (Roy) Villaronga

This didn't stop our current problem. We couldn't get any pilots to fly me, as the Executive Officer of the Company, in to take charge of the company and get Plummer out. The pea soup was too thick and dangerous to fly in. That didn't help with Division, the order was get Plummer out and do it now. Finally I found a Warrant Officer and crew who said they would get me and the supplies out there or die trying. Great thought since I had already tried it several times and agreed with the previous pilots, how in hell are we going to fly through the mountains in this gunk. Nonetheless we loaded the supplies, I jumped on and we were on our way.

We flew up Highway 1 at a little over 50 feet and when we reached the guide mark the pilot had chosen we turned to the West toward the mountains. The fog bank continued to cover the mountains and the company reported they were still socked in. The pilot then elevated the helicopter to around five thousand feet while constantly talking to the troops on the ground. Soon the company picked up the sound of the helicopter and began guiding us to their location. The problem remained, we still could see nothing, neither the ground nor the mountains. We were sitting on pins in needles thinking anytime we are going to meet a ridge head on. Finally, we received those well needed words, you are about 100 meters to our right and maybe a couple of 100 feet above us. By calling out corrections and bringing us down slowly we finally saw old terra firma about 10 feet below us. The pilot eased the aircraft down to the ground and the men began unloading much needed food and water from the helicopter. I reached over and shook the pilot's hand (for that matter I was so relieved I shook everyone's hand, including the copilot, crew chief, and gunner). I then jumped out.

The mountain had a small saddle in it and Plummer just happened to be on the opposite high ground from where we landed. Since I was replacing him until the new commander could join us we had to wait until he made his way over to the helicopter. He boarded quickly and without so much as a farewell, take care of the men, or even kiss my ass Lieutenant, he signaled to the pilot and the chopper lifted straight up turned to the East and was out of sight before I could turn and head towards the CP. After reaching the CP and meeting with 1st SGT Craig, I found they had hardly eaten anything for several days and had resorted to rationing out the little food they had. They had expected to be on the mountain for at most two days and then be picked up. When this did not happen they had no option except to dig up some of the least desirable canned rations they had tossed in the sump, such as fruit cake and some of the other less liked rations (Ham and Lima Beans comes to mind). At least by getting the log bird in they now had plenty of rations to eat.

CHAPTER 23

VILLARONGA TAKES CHARGE

The next morning we woke to breaking fog and soon thereafter Captain Raul (Roy) Villaronga arrived and took command just long enough to tell us to mount up, we were marching off the mountain, now called Starvation Mountain by the troops. Great, not only were the men getting of the mountain, but they now had to carry all the extra rations and equipment I had brought in the previous day. Ah, such is the life of an infantryman. After a several hour trek down the mountain we finally reached the rice paddies in the plain below.

While taking a break, Villaronga received word lift ships were inbound to our location. We were to be picked up and make an air assault near the hamlet of Gia Duc (1) in the Kim Son Valley area. The village of Gia Duc consisted of seven separate hamlets, each numbered, and was located about seven kilometers from the An Loa Valley, a known NVA/VC stronghold and staging area. There had been several reports of enemy sightings in the area and we were to search the area and attempt to locate them. We were also told we need not worry about going in to a hot LZ. We would be coming in from North to South and the higher ground immediately to the east of the landing zone was already secured by two Special Forces advisors and Company of ARVN troops who would provide security during our landing on the LZ.

Villaronga turned to me and said, "I've never made a combat assault. What is the normal protocol." I explained to him the first thing is to find out how many ships would be in each lift and how they were planning on landing for pickup (i.e., Heavy Right, Heavy Left, or Line). The open area we were in allowed for any of them to work. I then told him the Company Commander usually would be in the first lift, but suggested he not be in the lead helicopter, but rather the 2nd or 3rd ship. His chances are better if we end up going into a hot LZ. I then recommended the 3rd platoon led by Lt Roger Riffle be in the first lift, followed by the 1st Platoon, then the 2nd Platoon. The 4th platoon would bring up the rear. I said I would be with this lift so I could ensure we left no one on the pickup zone. He said that sounded good to him except he wanted me on the same helicopter as the command group. I objected saying you don't want the CO and the XO on the same chopper in case we run into trouble. After thinking about it he agreed, but said, "I still want you on the first lift." 1stSGT Craig would bring up the rear and make sure no one was left on the ground.

With this finalized, he then studied the map of the Gia Duc (1) area. There were two elevated areas to the North of the hamlet with a large rice paddy between them. The first lift on the ground would secure the higher ground to the west of the LZ. The second lift would then move to the east and relieve the ARVN troops and Special Forces Advisors to return to their compound. The next two lifts would join the first lift on the high ground to the west. Once all were in place the three platoons to the west would support the movement of the 1nd platoon as it moved south across a large rice paddy and enter the hamlet. Once secured the remainder of the company would move across and all would conduct a search of the hamlet.

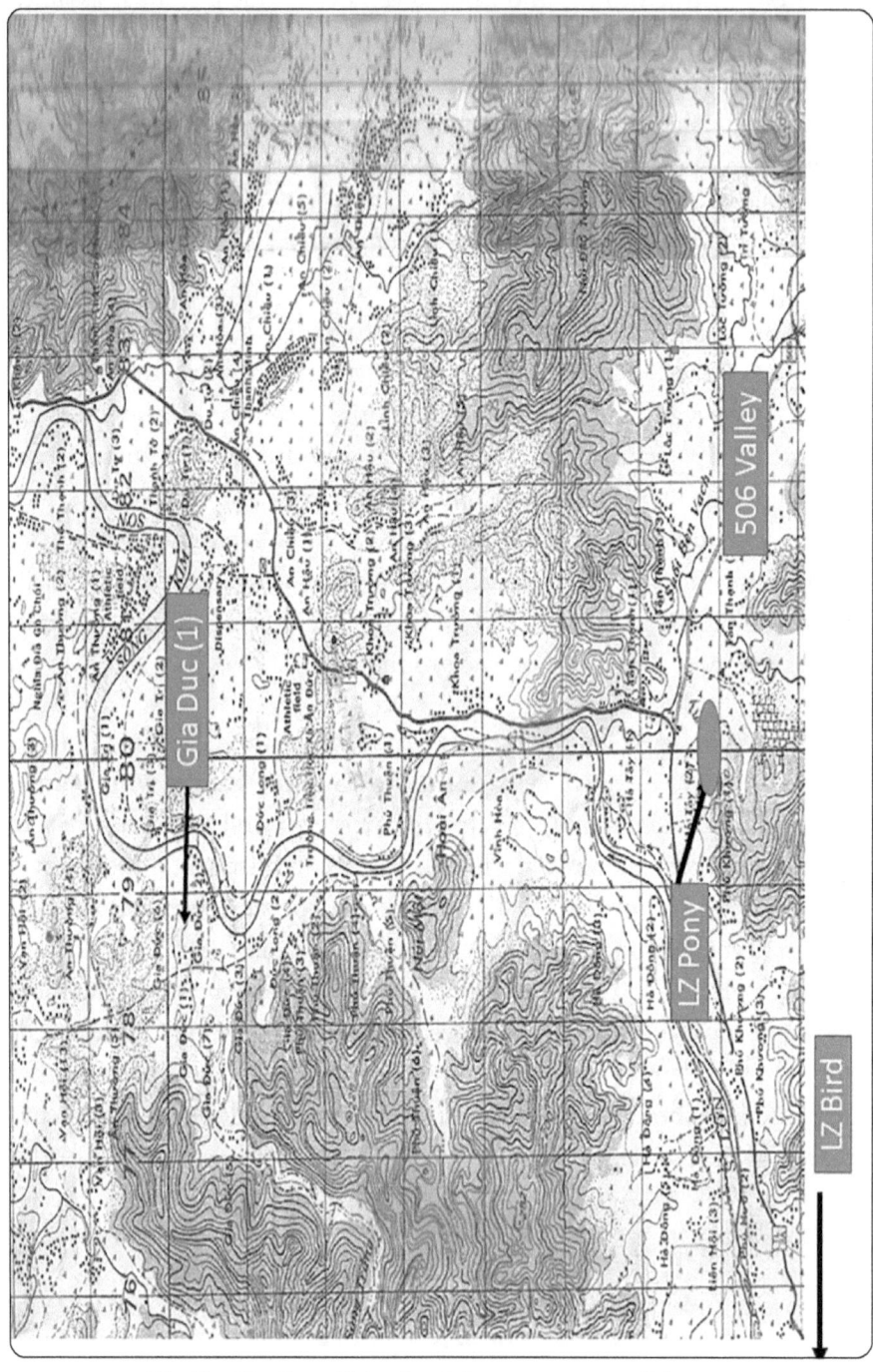

Fig 33. Gia Duc (1) in the right upper corner of the map

And the Tears Flowed

I thought, not a bad plan, and I told the Captain it sounded good. I then told 1ˢ SGT Craig he would be on the last lift to ensue no one was left behind. The pickup went without a hitch and after what seemed a short ride we came in from the north and landed as planned between the two small hills in the rice paddy just north of the hamlet. It was then Murphy's Law kicked in, "If anything can go wrong, it will". As we landed I saw no friendly forces on the hill to the east securing the LZ as we had been told and as we started for the high ground to the west through the flooded paddy we began receiving sniper fire from the Hamlet. Villaronga yelled for me to stay in the paddy and direct the second lift to go west vice east. Not an order I relished but I dropped behind a paddy dike laying in water and mud pending the arrival of the next two lifts. The sniper had stopped firing which I thought was great, except as the next ships started landing and I stood up shouting and motioning to the troops, he opened up again. I would motion with my arm for them to go left, drop down behind the dike, crawl a few yards, raise up again yelling and motioning for the arriving troops to go west towards the 3rd Platoon's location. After doing this several times they finally all heeded my directions and headed toward the troops already on the ground. The troops already to the west helped by firing towards the hamlet and finally the sniper ceased shooting. The next lift landed without opposition and it was easy for them and I to join the rest of the company. Once the Company was on the ground and in position, Villaronga ordered the 3rd platoon to assault across the paddy while the remainder of the company laid down a base of fire. The 3rd led by SFC Winfield Bledsoe, accomplished this without taking fire, and quickly secured a footing in the hamlet allowing the rest of the company to cross. The company quickly rounded up the occupants of the hamlet and moved them to the center of the hamlet where they were questioned. As usual the assembled crowd was devoid of young men, only women, small children and old men. No one knew anything and did not know who had fired at us. Their attitude toward us was not friendly, but then we had just conducted an air assault on their hamlet and moved in firing, probably scaring the hell out of them. A thorough search was made, but we found neither the sniper nor any weapons. We did find an individual who claimed he was a former ARVN soldier who had lost both legs and was confined to a small pallet with wheels which allowed him to maneuver around the hamlet. He also had proper papers, but for some reason I had an uneasy feeling that he was at least a VC sympathizer, although we could not prove it. We never did find out what happened to the "friendly forces" who were supposedly securing the LZ for us.

The Company then swept south from the hamlet and searched several other hamlets that made up the village and the surrounding areas for a little over a week, mainly to the south of Gia Duc (1). All turned out to be dry areas. No NVA or VC units were encountered and the villagers had no knowledge of any enemy forces in the area or were unwilling to say so. Nonetheless, if there had been any in the area they had simply disappeared. It was also during this time frame the mortar platoon was converted to a rifle platoon. Of course this was not without some tribulations. The men in the mortar platoon, although they knew basic infantry tactics, were trained to provide mortar support for the three other infantry platoons in the company. The very first night showed it would take a little time for them to adapt. We established a night defensive position with the three infantry platoons manning the perimeter. The previous mortar platoon was designated as the reserve reaction force and took up positions inside the perimeter. Around 2200 hours a burst of fire came from inside the perimeter. I immediately scrambled over to the fourth platoon's position to see why they fired. The response was "we heard movement to out front." My response was "no shit, you have the other three platoons in front of you." Luckily no one in front of them were injured, but needless to say there were a few really teed of infantrymen to their front.

Later in the month the company was flown back to LZ Hammond and assigned security detail in the vicinity of the battalion trains area on the west side of the perimeter. This allowed the men the comfort of being able to take showers, albeit with cold water, and then provided new sets of jungle fatigues and hot meals. I flew back to An Khe and picked up payroll for the troops. This job usually took a week or longer given the fact men were scattered all over, some on Hammond, others back in base camp, some in the hospital, and some on R&R who would be paid when they returned.

CHAPTER 24

PHAN THIET/TASK FORCE BYRD AND BACK TO JAPAN

On 7 November the Company was ordered back to Camp Radcliffe to refit and prepare to move south to Phan Thiet, a city located in the southeast corner of II Corps on the South China Sea. We were to join Task Force Byrd, a unit that had been formed to counter increased enemy action in Binh Thuan Province located in the southern portion of II Corps Tactical Zone. On 8 November the Company boarded C-130s for the trip south to LZ Betty and its airfield, located just south of Phan Thiet, the Province Capital and on 9 November came under the operational control of the 2/7th Cavalry whose Battalion Commander commanded Task Force Byrd.

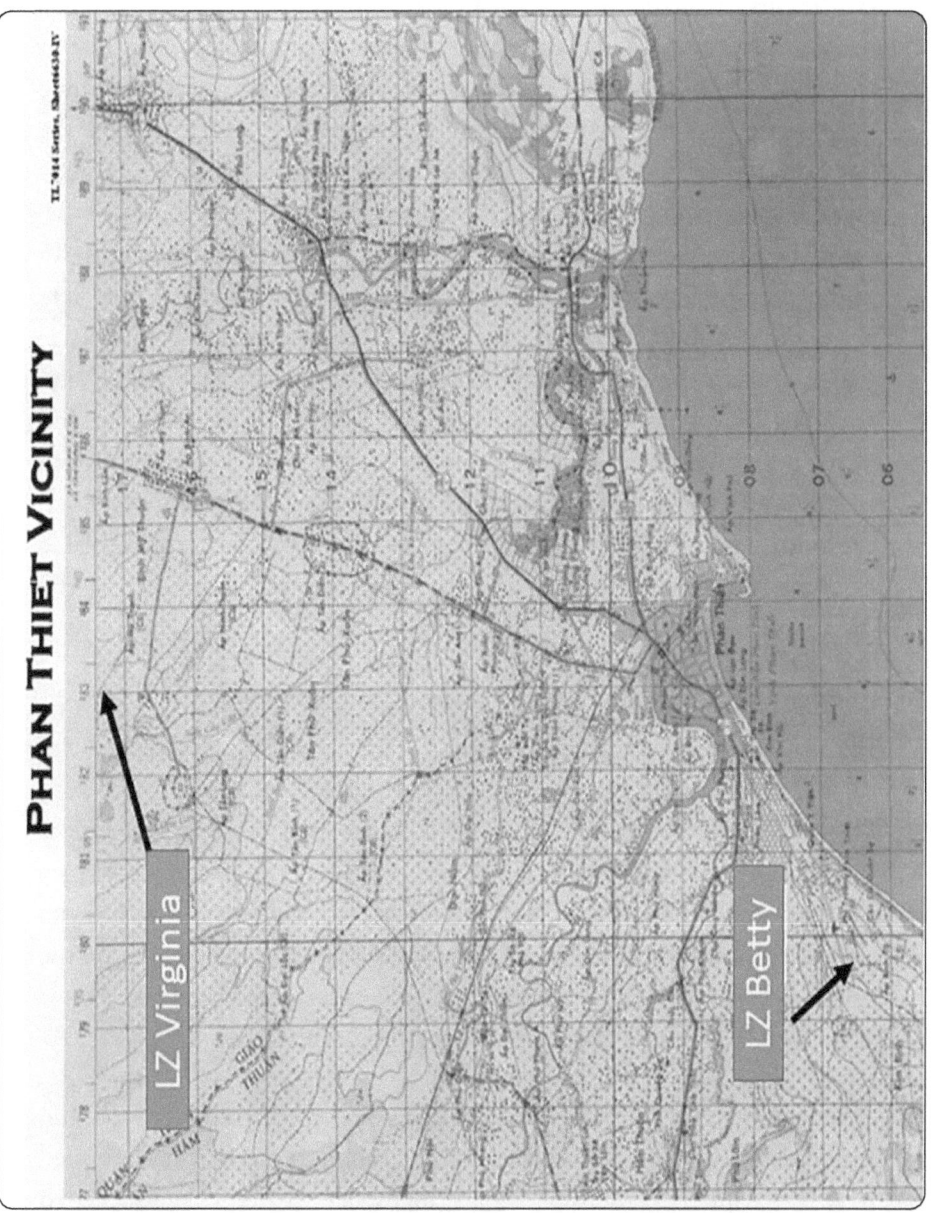

Fig 34. LZ Betty and Virginia to the Northeast

Task Force Byrd had been formed in August 1966. The main component was the 2/7th Cavalry. It included a battery of 105mm and a battery of 155mm howitzers as well as UH-1 helicopters on LZ Betty. The mission of the task force was to conduct search and destroy missions throughout the Province. The company arrived and initially assumed duty as perimeter defense of the airfield and LZ. Once settled the company was also assigned patrolling missions around the LZ to get a lay of the land and to work on defenses around the perimeter of the base. Soon thereafter we were moved to LZ Virginia an artillery base some 15 kilometers northwest of the city at coordinates BN815176. From here the company pulled perimeter security and ran platoon and squad size patrols during the day and ambush patrols at night. Very little action occurred. The various patrols did capture a number of local VC, but did not engage any main force VC units. On one patrol a newly assigned member, PFC Jerry Burnett, stepped on a Bouncing Betty mine which exploded basically waist high severely wounded him in both legs. He later died and was the only casualty from the company during the duration of duty with Task Force Byrd.

On one rotation back to LZ Betty the Company Commander allowed the troops passes to the city of Phan Thiet, a quaint University city on the coast, but which reeked from the smell of nuo'c mam (also known as Nuo'c Cha'm) a spicy fish sauce used to season a variety of Vietnamese dishes. Phan Thiet was a major producer of this spicy sauce. The fishermen would lay freshly caught fish on plastic covering the sidewalks of the streets until it basically rotted and then squeeze the juice from the fish into containers, add spices and then let if ferment. It actually tasted pretty good, once you got passed the smell.

After the first few days, passes were issued to several of our troops who immediately went into town and found an opium den where they tried to buy marijuana or heroin. When the owner refused they proceeded to berate the Vietnamese owner and patrons and then randomly fired their weapons into the air in an attempt to scare him. Needless to say the Vietnamese National Police arrived almost immediately and arrested

And the Tears Flowed

the three individuals. Captain Villaronga assigned me the odious task of going in to the city and pleading with the Police Chief to release the three to my custody. After some haggling, he released them with the warning they were not allowed back into Phan Thiet. I assured him this would not be a problem. The Task Force Commander made it even plainer; Phan Thiet was now off limits to all troops except those entering town on official business. Needless to say, the 1/8th troops were not very well liked for the remainder of our stay in Phan Thiet.

Also, during our stay as part of the Task Force, I was granted an R&R to Tokyo. I looked with pleasure to the trip knowing I would again spend most of my time with Miyoko as the R&R Center was located at Camp Zama. I returned to base camp in An Khe, picked up the few civilian clothes I had, then with others selected for R&R, was flown to Nha Trang. Surprisingly I met up with the same Warrant Officer pilot who had flown me and the supplies to Starvation Mountain in October. As I recall his first name was Jim, but do not remember his last name. We renewed acquaintances, had a few drinks and then sat together as we flew to Yokoto AFB via a commercial airline. On arrival we were bussed to the Camp Zama reception area, where we received our indoctrination on the rules for R&R. The most important one I remember was the Sergeant saying to the troops, "As you go through the front gates heading for Tokyo or Yokohama, be advised you will see some of the most beautiful ladies you will ever lay eyes upon. They will tell you they know the perfect bar to start your R&R at. He then said look around at your buddies, because at least 25% of them will take these ladies up on their offer. The next morning we will meet these guys at the gate and they will all be broke. He also warned not to run tabs in any of the bars, but to pay cash every time a drink was ordered. It seems some bars in Japan can charge you exorbitant rates if you run a tab, but must accept the posted price if you pay for each drink. They will then spend the rest of their R&R here at Camp Zama playing pool or basketball at the recreation center." He then dismissed us to our seven days of sex and libations.

My Warrant friend and I shook hands as we departed Zama, he heading for Tokyo, I to Miyoko's home. As I drove away in the taxi I could see the R&R Sergeant was right. The women waiting outside the gate were gorgeous and were trolling the GIs as they left post. Some were already entering cabs with their ladies to parts unknown. I just smiled as I knew that the Sergeant was right and some of these guys would be back at the R&R Center the next morning.

I arrived at Miyoko's home where she met me with welcoming arms. We had remained in touch by mail after my return to Vietnam so she knew I would be arriving. We settled into a pretty natural routine. Stay in bed, make love, shower, dress and head for the bar around 1800 hours. Stay there and drink beer until closing. Head for the Korean restaurant for a meal then to the night club to dance, and then to her house for more lovemaking. Six days of bliss and relief from the horrors of war, then it all came crashing down. I had to return to the R&R Center at Zama for deployment back to the Vietnam. Neither Miyoko nor I was happy. As we said our good byes she said, "Bill, I do not think I will ever see you again." I tried to pass it off by telling her not to worry that I would be back, but knew in my heart the chances were unlikely. There were only few infantry slots at Zama and my chances were not very good at getting one of those slots. In addition, I also knew the life of an infantryman could be short. I had already witnessed that earlier in my tour. She cried as I boarded a taxi for Zama and the trip back to Vietnam. She was right, however; I never returned nor did I ever see her again, although we did communicate for several months after I left, but ultimately I wrote she was right and I would not be returning to Japan.

Sure enough when we entered the R&R Center for roll call, there were soldiers already sitting alone on one side of the room. The same Sergeant who had welcomed us on arrival greeted us again and said he hoped we had fun and enjoyed the splendor of Japan. He then pointed to the other side of the room and said "as I told you some of you wouldn't make it much past the front gate and all those pretty girls. These are those guys and they all spent the better part of their R&R here at Camp

Zama." Needless to say, there weren't a lot of smiles on their faces. We were then processed for return for Vietnam and boarded the plane that would carry us back to that hell hole.

We had a pretty uneventful flight back to Vietnam, except the C-130 flight back to Camp Radcliffe. As we were making our final approach to the airstrip the crew chief started bracing himself for the landing and started yelling "brace, brace he is coming in too fast, we're going to overshoot the airstrip." About that time the plane hit the airstrip and the pilot immediately began braking. We barreled down the runway and at the last moment the pilot was able to stop the aircraft just short of the end of the runway and a sharp drop off. The crew chief let out a loud sigh and said "fucking new pilot." He was clearly shook and as we exited the aircraft we could see why. The plane had torn up a large section of the perforated steel runway and the nose was just short of the ravine at the end of the runway.

The next morning I flew back to Phan Thiet to rejoin the company. The routine remained essentially the same. Air assaults and patrols seeking out the enemy, but with little luck. It almost appeared the main force units had gone to ground and the only thing we were running into were small local units of VC, at most squad sized. The highlight of our last few weeks with Task Force Byrd was a splendid hot Thanksgiving Dinner. The Officers and Senior NCOs manned the serving line and filled the paper plates of the troops with turkey, dressing, mashed potatoes with gravy and vegetables. I believe Apple pie was served for dessert. Even though we tried to provide the company with hot meals as often as we could, nothing compared to this meal. Routine patrolling again became the norm after Thanksgiving and finally on 12 Dec 1966 the company returned to An Khe and again fell under the command of the 1/8th Cav. Our mission with Task Force Byrd had come to end.

Fig 35. Phan Thiet: Myself, the CO, Platoon leaders and the Artillery Forward Observer

CHAPTER 25

OPERATION PERSHING, LZ GAVIN, AND THE BATTLE OF THE 506 VALLEY

The next several days were spent on stand down, refitting and replenishing supplies before moving again to the field. A Change of Command ceremony was held on the 14th with Lieutenant Colonel Ardie McClure taking over as Battalion Commander from Lieutenant Colonel Louisell who moved to the 3rd Brigade as Deputy Commander.

LTC Ardie McClure D Co, 12-66 to 6-67.
Photo taken 2-67

Fig 36. LTC Ardie McClure, CO 1/8th Bn

On the 16th, with Bravo Company in the lead, the Battalion moved by truck convoy from Camp Radcliffe to LZ Hammond. Departure was around 0700 and we closed on LZ Hammond around 1700 hours. Shortly thereafter Bravo led an air assault onto a ridge overlooking the Soui Ca Valley in the area known as the Crows Foot to an elephant grass and rock covered clearing surrounded by jungle

Fig 37. Air Assault on LZ Gavin (Depiction of Assault into Gavin)

The clearing was quickly dubbed LZ Gavin and could only accommodate two ships at a time. Landing and securing the LZ was not without incident. Two members of the company, were injured almost immediately by anti-personnel booby traps. One of the wounded was SP4 Jessie Smith, but I do not remember who the other WIA was.

And the Tears Flowed

Fig 38. SP5 Maurice "Doc" Waters tend the wounds on SP4 Jesse Smith

Fig 39. "Doc" Waters, CPT Raul Villaronga, and My RTO SP4 Lloyd Jack tend to U/I soldier on LZ Gavin

A cautious search of the area uncovered numerous punji stakes and a number of old fighting positions left by an enemy unit that had previously occupied the ridge. They had left their calling card. Both members were treated quickly by the company medic, SP5 Maurice Waters and my RTO Lloyd Jack, then evacuated on one of the following lifts. Once the LZ was secured CPT Villaronga sent one platoon up the ridge toward the crest and another towards the valley to make sure whomever had been there previously had evacuated the area. The first patrol turned up a recently-used platoon-sized base camp about 300 meters east of the LZ. They estimated it was about 2-3 weeks old. The remainder of the company began clearing and enlarging the LZ for the arrival of the Battalion Headquarter element and a battery from the 2/19 Artillery who would provide artillery support for the other companies of the battalion who would begin operations in the Soui Ca Valley and the surrounding mountainous terrain. We encountered no resistance while accomplishing this relocation and by 1800 hours all occupants of the LZ were firmly entrenched for the night. Bravo found it to be a short stay.

The next day, December 17, while securing the Battalion Headquarters and the artillery battery on Gavin, Bravo Company was alerted to move to assist the 1/12th Cav who were heavily engaged with an enemy force in the 506 Valley (also part of the Crows Foot area and was named such because route 506 traversed through the valley). At 1350 hours the 1st element of B Company air assaulted just west of the hamlets of Thach Long (1) and (2) and were placed under the operational control of the 1/12th Cav.

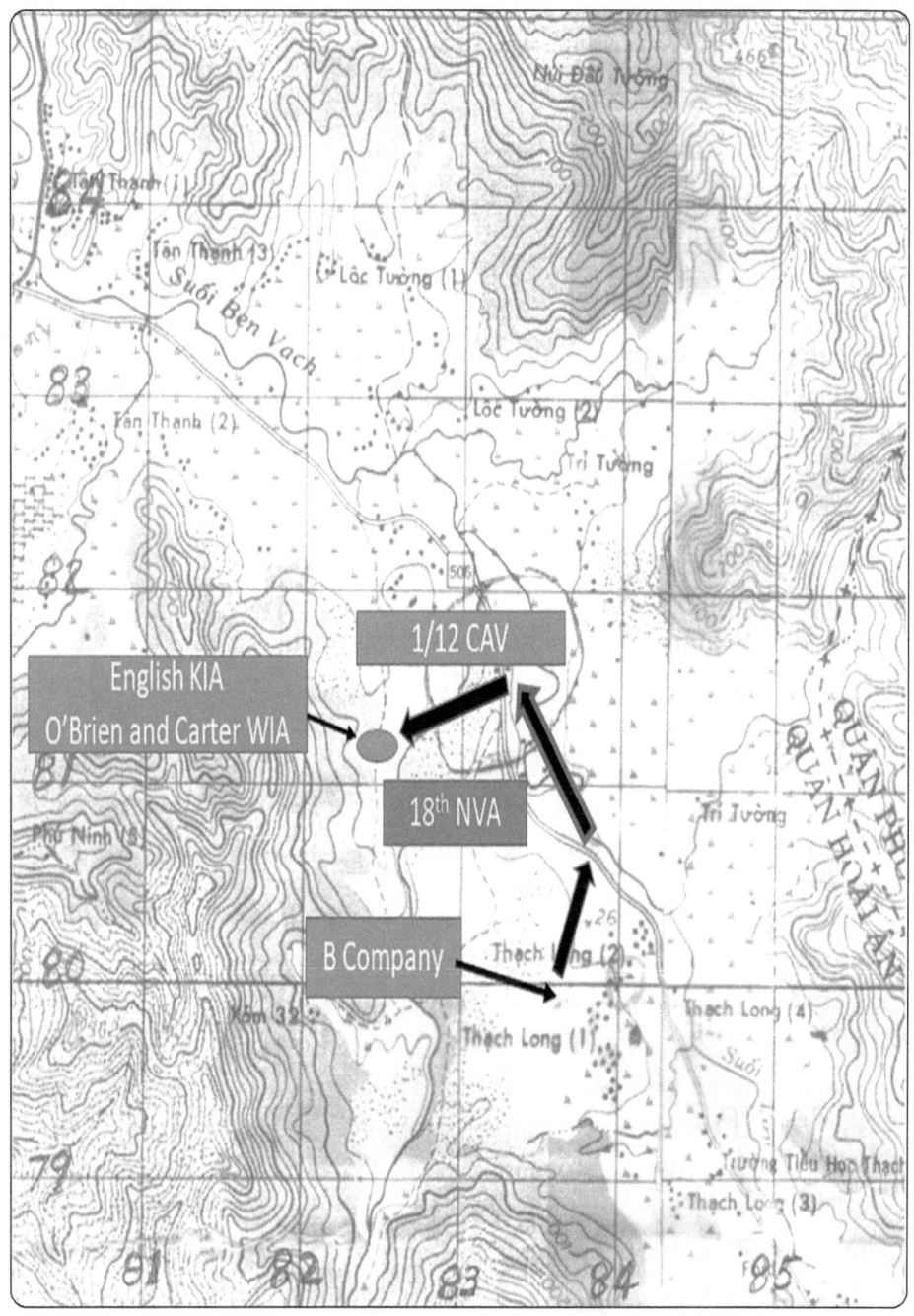

Fig 40. Battle of the 506 Valley

By 1650 hours all elements of B Company were on the ground. I arrived on the last lift from LZ Gavin and was told by the pilot of the Huey that we were going into a hot LZ. He stated he would touch down briefly and everyone was to exit the A/C as quickly as possible. As we approached the LZ where the company had established a perimeter I could see 5 or 6 attack helicopters firing and being fired at by green tracers probably six to eight hundred meters to the North of our company's position. I thought several were shot down and later confirmed this was the case. I also found out that almost every other gunship had been hit by enemy gunfire while supporting the $1/12^{th}$. As we began our final approach into the Company's position I jumped from the chopper at about 15 feet above the paddy since we had been told it was a hot LZ and landed in a water filled rice paddy sinking almost to my waist. The others on the Huey, quickly followed suit. I had seen the C.O. as we were coming in and after extracting myself made it to his position. He was smiling wryly and asked why I jumped from the aircraft when I did. On explaining we were told the LZ was hot, he laughed and stated "we haven't received a single round, but the $1/12^{th}$ to our North were in extremely heavy contact with a large enemy force and had taken severe casualties, both killed and wounded. Our initial mission was as a blocking force to prevent the enemy force, later identified as the 18th NVA Regiment, from escaping to the South.

Once the entire company was on the ground we were ordered by the $1/12^{th}$ Battalion Commander, LtCol Eggers, to move north and join up with his units on the ground. We began moving reluctantly parallel to and on Route 506, after our CO protested vehemently to Eggers. This in our opinion was not a good idea, since the enemy force was somewhere between our current position and his rifle companies locations. He ordered us to move anyway. Their southernmost company was in close proximity to BR835812, or a little over a kilometer north of our position. We began moving as ordered and as we approached the southern portion of their location near dusk they mistook us for the enemy and opened fire with small arms and a machine gun. Luckily no one was hit and Villaronga was quickly able to get them to cease fire.

We then linked up with their A Company and it was patently evident they had been hit hard. Numerous bodies and wounded lay sprawled within their perimeter. After meeting with their company commander Bravo Company was directed to move West/Southwest about 200 to 300 meters and establish our own perimeter for the remainder of the night. By then it was totally dark but we moved as ordered.

I believe when we established our perimeter it was located in the vicinity of BR 821811 or about 200 yards from the 1/12th perimeter. A trail ran through the area Villaronga selected for our company's position. We were generally southwest of the 1/12th perimeter. More upsetting however; we found the bodies of nine American soldiers along or near the trail. They had evidently walked into a well concealed L-shaped ambush and apparently no one from the 1/12th had attempted to retrieve the bodies. One young black man, although wounded, had crawled away from the trail and sought refuge under a bush. He evidently died of his wounds when no help was forthcoming. We retrieved his body and laid him with the others who had been killed in the ambush and near the position Villaronga selected as our command post for the night. We were, to say the least, pissed that the 1/12th Company had sent us into a location they had been in contact with the enemy and where they without a doubt knew had taken casualties.

After we secured the area Villaronga called the platoon leaders to his location to assign positions for the night and to give them a general briefing on what we would be doing in the morning. They had no sooner assembled than someone to the east of our position fired an M-79 grenade into our location. I had heard the pop of the M-79 as it fired and yelled "get down", but before we could it hit a tree above us and exploded. SP4 Mark English was killed immediately when a piece of shrapnel hit him in the base of his skull.

Fig 41. PFC Mark English

SP4 Pat O'Brien was severely hit by shrapnel in both legs to the extent it severed one of them completely off and severely damaged the other. PFC Robert Carter who was next to O'Brien also sustained shrapnel wounds in both legs. Surprisingly no one else suffered injuries even though there were at least 15 others in the immediate vicinity of the explosion. We believed the round was fired from the 1/12th positions, but could not rule out that it may have been an enemy soldier that had possibly captured the M-79, heard our movement and fired on us. It mattered not, we had still lost Mark English even though Sp5 Maurice Waters and several other medics worked feverishly on him as well as the two other wounded.

Fig 42. SP4 Pat O'brien and SP4 Mark English Shortly before the 506 Valley Battle

Fig 43. SP4 Robert Carter

The company RTO, George Michael, immediately called for a medevac, but they refused to come because of darkness, the heavy fighting that had taken place earlier in the day, and the possibility that enemy forces were still in the vicinity posing a risk to them. A lone Huey (UH-1) log ship pilot heard our call for assistance and didn't hesitate to land and take our casualties out. I believe he and our head medic, Maurice Waters was instrumental in saving O'Brien's life. We found out later O'Brien did lose both legs. Carter later rejoined the company and completed his tour of duty.

Once the evacuation was complete we solidified our position for the remainder of the night; then helped the 1/12th police their dead the following morning; and then swept the area south of the 1/12th location in an attempt to locate the enemy force with negative results. The 506 Valley is located in the Crows Foot area of Binh Dinh Province, was a strong sanctuary for the Viet Cong and the NVA, and an area where we saw numerous small unit actions during Operations Thayer I/II, Irving, and Pershing.

CHAPTER 26

CHRISTMAS CEASE FIRE AND LZ BIRD

We remained under the operational control of the 1/12th until December 21st then returned to LZ Gavin and resumed platoon size patrols around Gavin. On the 23rd all elements of Bravo Company returned to the LZ for the Christmas cease fire. Christmas Eve the Company Command Group partook of a delicious dinner of C-rations. We each added a can of different C's to a pot, mixed them all together added an ample helping of hot peppers and Tabasco sauce, then heated the mixture with heat tablets. The goulash type meal actually turned out to be pretty good and we supplemented an after meal coffee with a splash of rum from a bottle that Captain Villaronga had stashed in his rucksack. We were all pretty melancholy as our thoughts turned to families back home wishing we could be there with them. Someone on the perimeter began singing "Silent Night" in an unbelievable beautiful voice and before long everyone on the LZ joined in before retiring for the night. We did notice lights moving north along a road in the valley below us, but took no action to engage since we were still under a cease fire order.

Christmas day was just another routine day for us. It was unusual inasmuch as the artillery had fallen silent and only one platoon sent out several squad size patrols around the LZ just to make sure Charlie wasn't trying to pull anything. That evening a hot meal and a beer for each man was sent out from the supply train at LZ Hammond. I seem to recall it was sliced turkey with mashed potatoes and gravy. Regardless it sure tasted good. Of course, thoughts for most were on home and families who would be celebrating Christmas without their sons or husbands on hand.

On the 26th the company air assaulted into LZ Clause around 1200 hours then swept back to LZ Gavin located to the southeast, again as a precautionary measure to make sure Charlie was up to no good during the cease fire. The company found a two-week-old base camp and one dead VC during the sweep. We closed on Gavin around 1600 hours where we again took up perimeter security. The artillery remained silent as we continued to observe the cease fire. For the remainder of the evening the company took the opportunity to clean weapons and write letters to loved ones back home. In all a very quiet day.

All this changed on the early morning hours of December 27th when at approximately 0100 hours we heard explosions in the distance. It was puzzling since the cease fire was still in effect, but we quickly found out through radio communications a full scale attack by a large NVA/VC force was taking place against two artillery batteries, B Battery 2/19th and C Battery 6/16th Artillery on LZ Bird. An understrength rifle company, C Company 1/12th Cavalry, secured the perimeter located some 18 kilometers to the northwest of our position. Incoming reports were sketchy for the most part, but we knew the friendlies were in serious trouble. We also knew that our former artillery forward observer, 1st Lieutenant Mike Livengood was on Bird in charge of the Fire Direction Center which was cause for some concern on my part. We had become close when he served with Bravo Company as a forward observer. As we monitored the ongoing situation we learned the attackers had overwhelmed the friendlies, had captured the 6/16th 155mm artillery pieces and were pushing the attack on the 2/19th 105mm positions. The commander of the 2/19th ordered the remaining guns to lower their barrels and fire two bee hive canister rounds into the attacking force.

The results were immediate and deadly. The NVA force was stopped in their tracks with devastating casualties and those surviving immediately fell back and withdrew from the battle. The attack on LZ Bird was over for the most part. The men on the LZ had suffered 28 KIAs and 67 WIAs. The 22ND NVA Regiment lost 266 men in the attack, and possibly more. Other U.S. units from the 1/12th and units from the 1/5th Cav were sent to reinforce and take care of the casualties that littered the LZ at first light. SGT Delbert Jennings, C 1/12th was awarded the Medal of Honor for his actions during the attack.

CHAPTER 27

BATTLE OF GIA DUC

On LZ Gavin, Bravo Company, which had been designated as the 1st Brigades Quick Reaction force during the LZ Bird attack, was placed on standby in mid-morning of the 27th for a possible air insertion northeast of LZ Bird to intercept any NVA forces moving in that direction seeking to gain sanctuary in the An Lao Valley, a long known NVA/VC stronghold, approximately 15-16 kilometers from LZ Bird. Just after 1300 hours the word came that lift ships were inbound. We would be deployed about 1500 meters north of the hamlet of Gia Duc (1), the same hamlet we had air assaulted into in late October. Only three platoons and the command group would take part in the assault. The 2nd Platoon had been sent on patrol earlier that morning and would be assigned to providing security on LZ Gavin when they returned later that afternoon. They then would be replaced by Alpha Company and would join us as soon as they could. It turned out this would not happen for several days.

At approximately 1400 hours the first five helicopters departed Gavin. It consisted of the 3rd Platoon, commanded by 2nd Lt Roger Riffle, and the Command Group. They would be followed by the 1st Platoon, led by 1st Lt Daniel Hennessy, and the 4th Platoon, led by 1st Lt Lamont Finch, who would bring up the rear. All were experienced leaders and respected by the men they led. The landing zone selected was about one and a half kilometer north of Gia Duc (1) on a boulder strewn, slightly elevated hill just to the west of the hamlet of An Thuong (4) and just south of Van Hoi (13). Charlie Company went in first and moved to secure the hamlet of Van Hoi (2) and the LZ for Bravo. The insertion went as planned except when jumping from the Huey -- about 6 feet from the ground -- I landed on a fairly large boulder, slipped and landed hard on my lower back. Although extremely painful I opted to stay with the company rather than being evacuated. Once all elements were on the ground, Bravo Company moved east towards An Thuong (4) and crossed a wide dirt trail running north to south capable of handling vehicular traffic. It showed signs of heavy foot traffic usage.

Charlie Company as noted had air assaulted into the same boulder strewn LZ previous to our landing and proceeded to move to the vicinity of the hamlet of Van Hoi (2) to the north of us, where they would set up for the night. They would then move east to the Kim Song (river) and follow our 1st Platoon as it moved south towards Gia Duc in the morning. Meanwhile, Villaronga directed Lt Finch and the 4^{tst} platoon to establish a position where his platoon could observe the heavily used trail. He did so by deploying his men on the high ground to the west of the trail. The remainder of the company moved on to An Thuong, where a search of the hamlet was conducted. As usual there were many women and old men, but a definite lack of young men in the hamlet. Following the search the command group and the 3rd platoon moved just to the south of the hamlet and took up a defensive position while the 1st continued toward the Kim Son to the east where they would spend the night observing the river for any enemy trying to use the river to move north.

Our purpose was to cut off any attempt by the NVA/VC to make it to the sanctuary of the An Loa valley some 5-6 kilometers north from our locations. Shortly after taking up positions for the night the 4th platoon intercepted a group of suspected enemy soldiers moving north on the road. None were armed, but all were of military age and when searched their shoulders showed signs of having carried load bearing equipment. They were escorted to the CP and Battalion was notified.

They informed that they would send a Chinook Helicopter in the morning and the prisoners were to be escorted to the POW Compound at LZ Hammond for interrogation. We settled in for the night with no further action, but remained on high alert.

The next morning as promised we were notified a Chinook was inbound to take the POWs. While waiting the company had breakfast and prepared to move as soon as they were rid of the prisoners. Captain Villaronga designated myself, my RTO Lloyd Jack, and several other men who had minor injuries from the air assault to escort the POWs to compound at Hammond. Shortly thereafter the Chinook landed, picked up the prisoners and the escorts and headed for LZ Hammond. The company then began moving south at 0945 towards the hamlet of Gia Duc (1). As related by Captain Villaronga he put the company in an inverted V-formation with 1st platoon on the left nearest the river and 3rd platoon on the right maneuvering in proximity to the road. The Command Group and 4th platoon brought up the rear.

They proceeded in this manner until just after noon when they reached high ground overlooking a rice paddy fronting Gia Duc (1). As they approached, Villaronga ordered the 1st and 3rd platoons to conduct flanking movements on the hamlet from the east and west with 4th platoon in a position on high ground in the middle overlooking the rice paddy to support either with fire, if necessary.

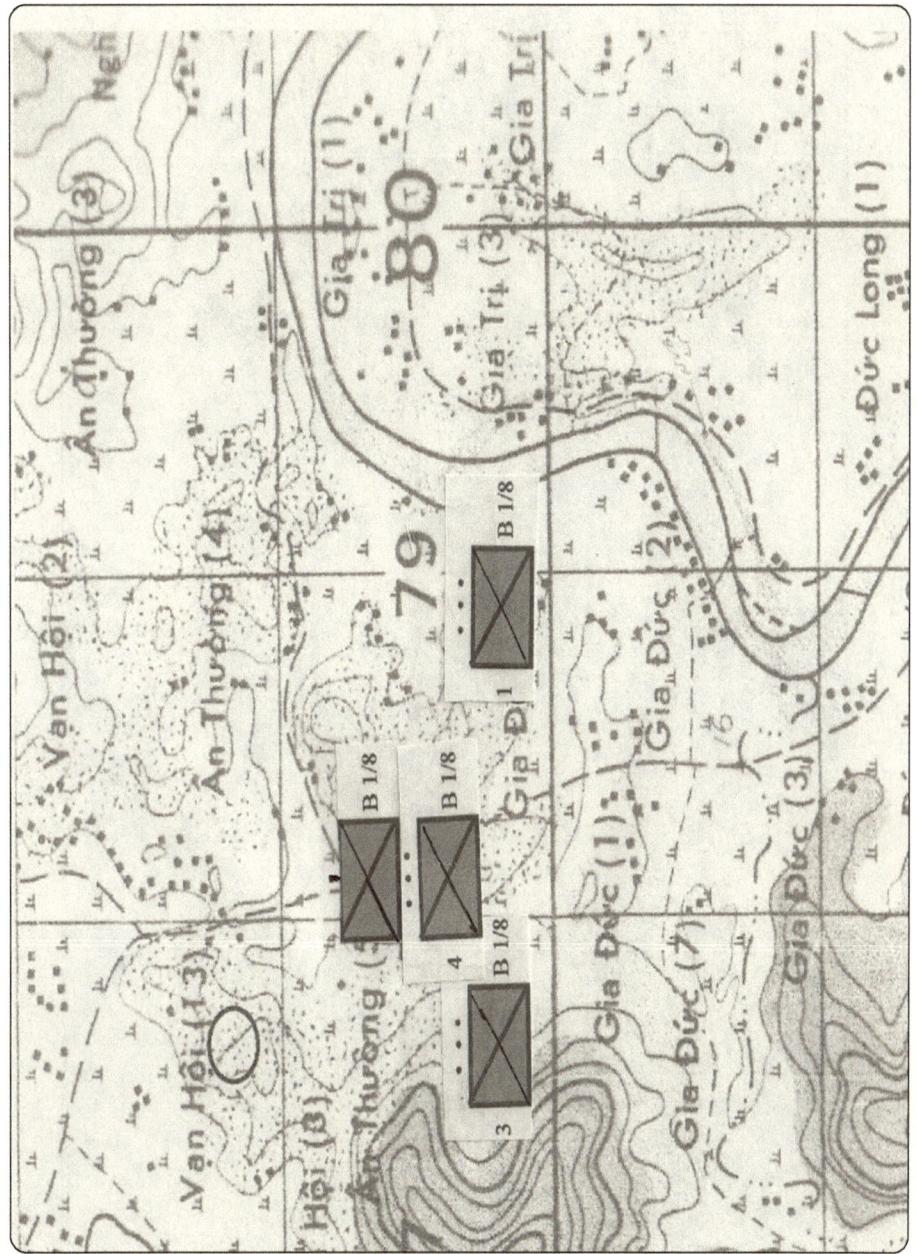

Fig 44. Movement to Contact Gia Duc (1)

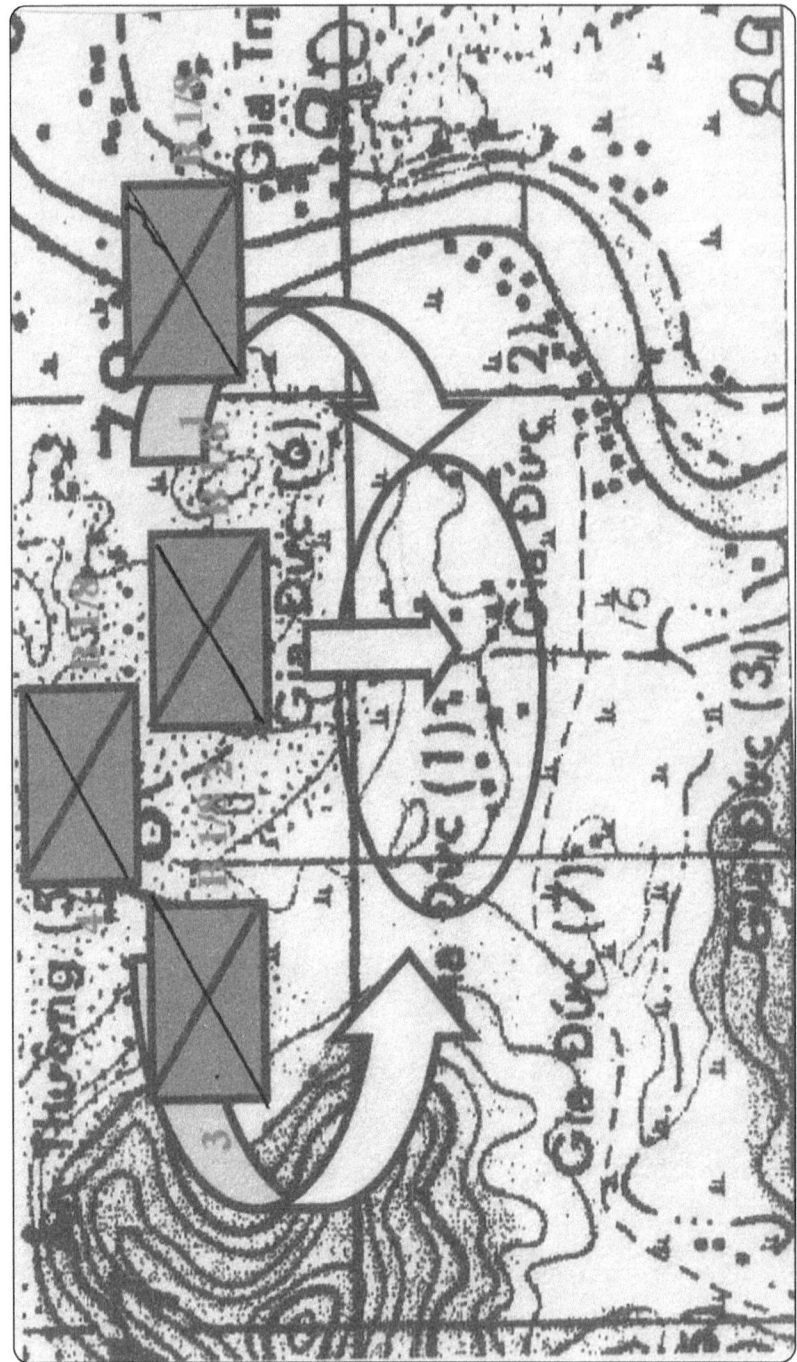

Fig 45. Attack on Gia Duc(1)

The 1st platoon, near the river, had to cross a rice paddy approximately 150-200 meters wide to reach the hamlet, while the 3rd maneuvered through a wood line and heavy underbrush near the base of a mountain ridge which sloped toward Gia Duc. As the 3rd platoon moved towards the northwestern edge of the hamlet, Villaronga and members of the 4th Platoon noted a flurry of activity in the hamlet. They initiated fire on the hamlet when they saw a number of individuals dressed in what appeared to be NVA uniforms moving in the hamlet.

To the west an NVA soldier jumped up in front of Sp4 Ernie Mendez, who was with the 3rd platoon, and ran toward the hamlet. Ernie yelled a warning to SGT Jerry Diersing to his left, but neither were able to get a shot before the NVA soldier vanished in the heavy underbrush as he ran toward the hamlet. Lt Riffle ordered the platoon on line and as they continued toward the hamlet they were met by extremely heavy fire from a well camouflaged and concealed enemy force in a hedgerow at the northern edge of the hamlet. Mendez was hit almost immediately and went down fatally injured. Ernie had only days left in country when he lost his life. He was an excellent experienced soldier, and extremely well liked by all in the company.

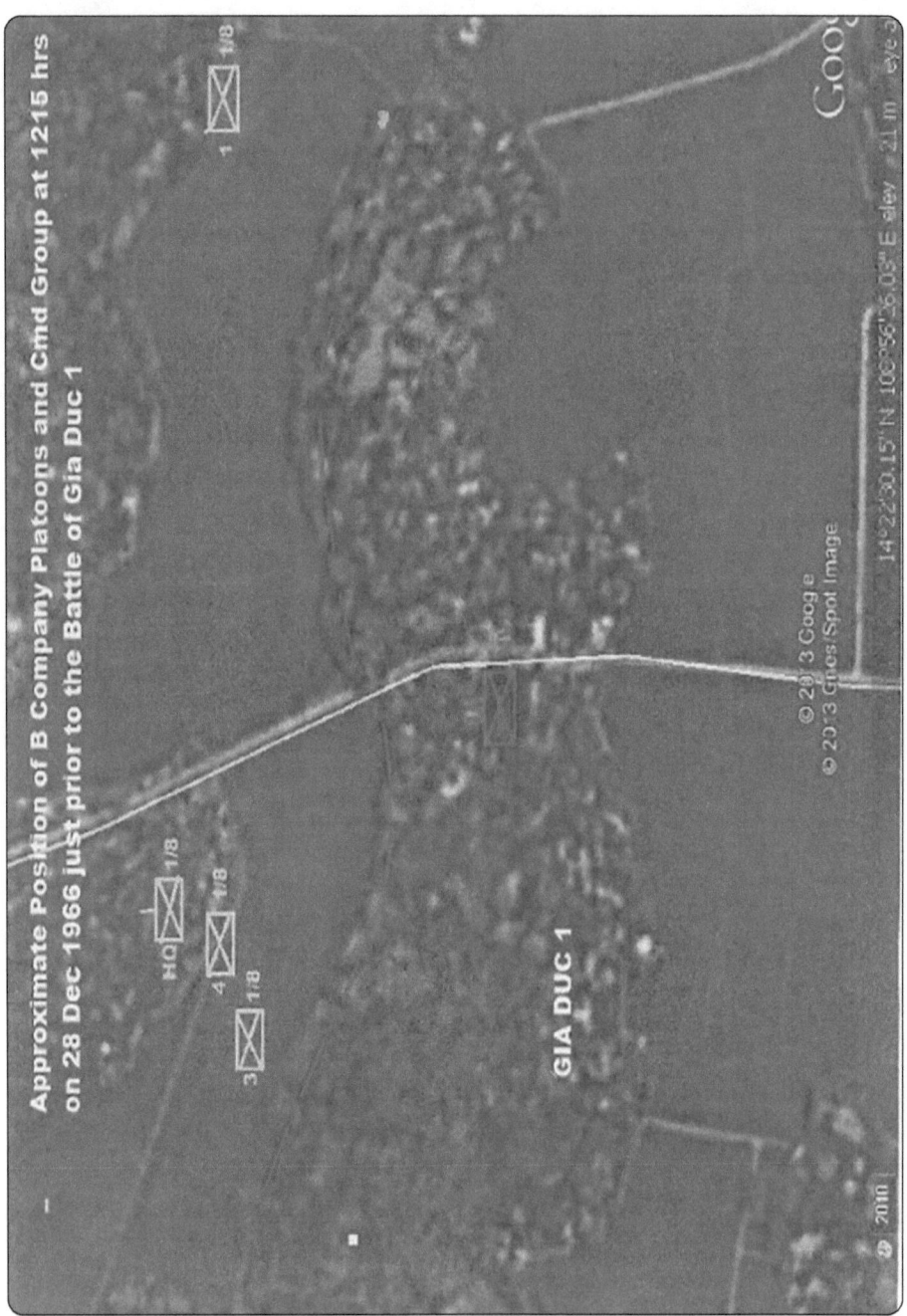

Fig 46. Platoon Positions Just Prior to the Attack on Gia Duc(1)

Fig 47. SP4 Erineo (Ernie) Ernie Mendez

The 3rd platoon was now pinned down and unable to maneuver against what they now knew to be a well-armed and well trained enemy force. Sergeant Diersing who had been walking point was pinned down as he took cover behind a tree and saw several other members of the platoon take hits and go down from the heavy fire being directed at them.

Fig 48. SGT Jerry Diersing

He noticed one man had been shot through the neck, but didn't know who the individual was, only that he desperately needed help. He crawled to him knowing the injury was bad. He attempted to stop the bleeding by inserting a finger in the wound, but was unable to stem the flow of blood. The individual was able to tell Diersing he was from Downey, California and was a medic. He was heavily tattooed on his arms, and also told Diersing he had been a Hells Angel before being drafted. At the same time SP5 Maurice Waters, the Company's head medic was moving toward them to assist. As he removed his M5 bag to treat the man he took a bullet to his chest with such force it knocked him of his feet. The round hit him just above the heart and ricocheted of a rib and exited under his arm. Although seriously wounded Maurice survived, the man with the neck wound did not. (Note: Years later after much research Maurice and I learned the unidentified man was PFC Walter Wonnacott. He had been sent to the company as a replacement medic during the battle only to be killed himself as he attempted to join the 3rd platoon while under fire).

Fig 49. PFC Walter Wonnacott, Medic

Heavy fire had also erupted to the left where the 1st platoon had come under intense fire, including at least one 50 Caliber machine gun as they crossed the rice paddy. The situation for that platoon was dire as most of the platoon members were caught in the rice paddy and were unable to move forward or retreat back to the wood line on the higher ground near the river. Pinned down they could only hope that help would soon arrive.

Lt Lamont Finch meanwhile began moving the 4th platoon to support the 3rd platoon. They had barely begun their maneuver to the right flank of the 3rd platoon when he was shot in the head and killed instantly by a sniper in a tree. Almost immediately PSGT Lonnie Barber was also killed by a shot to the head in the opening moments of the maneuver as enemy snipers took out the leadership of the 4th Platoon.

Fig 50. 1st Lt Lamont Finch, Platoon Leader, 4th Platoon

Fig 51. PSG Lonnie Barber, 4th Platoon

Several others men from the platoon were also killed in the initial burst of fire from the hamlet and others were wounded by the deadly well aimed and intense fire. Among those killed were Sp4 Dennis Spahn, and PFC James Pawlak. Spahn, another popular soldier, was also nearing his end of tour.

Fig 52. SP4 Dennis Spahn, PFC James Pawlak, 4th Platoon

To the east the 1st Platoon, still trapped in the rice paddy near the river, were also taking heavy casualties including Dan Hennessy who was cut down by enemy fire as he tried to rally his men.

Fig 53. 1st Lt Daniel Hennessy, Platoon Leader, 1st Platoon

PSGT Donald Brown, a former member of the Golden Knights Parachute Team, who had not yet entered the rice paddy assumed command of the platoon. Most of the men who had entered the rice paddy had either been killed or were wounded by the intense enemy fire. Among those killed were SP4 Eric Brannfors, SP4 Carl Mercer, PFC Richard Jacobs and CPL Douglas Hoag.

Fig 54. SP4 Brannfors, SP4 Mercer, Cpl Hoag, PFC Jacobs

Captain Villaronga had reported to Battalion that the company was in deep trouble and LTC Ardie McClure responded quickly by moving Charlie Company, who had been following the 1st platoon, up to support Bravo in the attack and also ordered Delta Company to air assault to the south of Gia Duc Village in the vicinity of Phu Thuan (3) about two kilometer south of the ongoing battle. As they landed around 1400 hours they were engaged immediately by another enemy force located in Phu Thuan. Five men, PFC Otto Baumann, PFC Douglas Fenney, SP4 Stephen Finney, PFC Daniel Mobley, and 1st SGT Joseph Moore were killed during the assault before Delta Company gained the upper hand as the remainder of the enemy force vanished into the surrounding mountains.

Lt Neal Laughy, the artillery forward observer assigned to Bravo Company was calling in devastating artillery strikes on the hamlet of Gia Duc (1). He continued to do so throughout the battle and well into the night. Gunships also attacked the hamlet time and time again as nightfall was fast approaching. Members of Charlie Company came to the aid of the 1st platoon and began retrieving the KIA and wounded for evacuation. Log ships delivered much needed supplies and Medevacs began extracting the wounded. The battle continued into the night and by that time the friendly units involved had virtually surrounded the hamlet of Gia Duc (1). Air strikes were called in and flew several sorties on the hamlet. Some of Bravo's 1st Platoon were still in the rice paddy either wounded or dead. During the night single gunshots could be heard coming from the area where these men were last seen just short of the hamlet, indicting some may have been executed where they lay, this even though artillery fired illumination flares throughout the night.

On the morning of the 29th Bravo, led by Captain Villaronga, again maneuvered the company toward Gia Duc and were finally able to enter the hamlet with only minimal opposition. They found Lt Hennessey's body as well as several others from the 1st Platoon who were killed on the edge or just short of the hamlet. A thorough search uncovered successive and connecting trench lines around and within the hamlet, trenches that had not existed when the company entered the hamlet in late October. Spider holes and independent fighting holes were also dispersed throughout. The company uncovered a tunnel leading to a fairly large underground room with maps annotating the plan of attack on LZ Bird. Other documents identified the attacking unit as the 22nd

NVA Regiment. Also found were personal belongings of some of the 1/12th troops and the artillerymen who lost their lives on Bird.

Interrogation of the villagers confirmed the 22nd NVA had been in the hamlet and other hamlets that made up the village of Gia Duc for at least a week prior to the attack on the Bird. The plan was well organized and, there is no question it would have been successful and the LZ overrun, had it not been for the resourcefulness of the artillerymen of the 2/19th who lowered their gun barrels to parallel and fired beehive rounds into the charging enemy soldiers who had penetrated the defensive perimeter and were near to accomplishing their mission of overrunning and destroying the firebase and all personnel on it. Throughout the remainder of the afternoon and evening other 1st Cav units assaulted into the area in pursuit of the fleeing enemy force and the 1/8th companies who had been involved in the action on the 28th began the odious task of evacuating the remaining dead and wounded as well as being resupplied. No further contact by the 8th Cav was established that day against the remnants of the 22nd NVA. It was as if they vanished into thin air.

CHAPTER 28

GRAVES REGISTRATION AND OPERATION THAYER II

In the meantime, SGT Charles Allen and I had been dispatched to the Division Graves Registration Detachment to identify those from Bravo Company who were killed on the 28th. This was, without a doubt, one of the hardest things I have ever had to do. To see and identify friends and soldiers who I had been with, joked with, and ate with just hours, days, and months before were now lying dead waiting to be identified by Allen and me before being prepared for shipment back to the United States to their loved ones. The first body I recalled was Sp4 Eric Brannfors, followed in no particular order by 1Lt Lamont Finch, 1Lt Daniel Hennessy, PSG Lonnie Barber, Cpl Douglas Houg, Pfc Richard Jacobs, Sp4 Erineo Mendez, Sp4 Carl Mercer, Pfc James Pawlak, and Sp4 Dennis Spahn. Looking at these brave young men brought a flood of tears to my eyes and the memory still haunts me to this day. I can't say enough about the men of the Graves Registration Detachment who did this every day. After completion of identifying the men of Bravo Company we returned to the Battalion trains area on LZ Hammond and on the next resupply flight I rejoined the Company in Gia Duc.

On the 30th Major General Norton, CG, 1st Cav Division flew into Gia Duc to congratulate the Company on a job well done. I met him as his command chopper landed. Norton had commissioned me when

And the Tears Flowed

I graduated from Officer Candidate Class 10-64 in December 1964. I would like to think he remembered me, but in all likelihood he had been forewarned on approach that I would meet him on landing and take him to our Company Headquarters location. After a quick briefing by the Company Commander he was escorted around the hamlet to see for himself the devastation we had wrought on the hamlet as well as the bodies of NVA/VC we had recovered. He then met with most of the men manning the perimeter or cleaning the battlefield. After about a 45 minute tour of the area he shook the hands of several of the officers, NCOs and men of the Command Group and with a heartfelt well done departed the area.

Also flying in was the Division Surgeon, a full Colonel and a medical doctor, who planned a two day stay with us. He expressed concern and even outrage about the number of troops in the company who had developed trench foot over the past few months during the Monsoon season stating the men were evidently not taking care of themselves and their feet properly. Since Captain Villaronga had already planned a patrol to search a hamlet to the southeast of Gia Duc along the river, he invited the Surgeon and several of his straphangers to come along so they could get a feel of what an infantryman goes through while on patrol. The surgeon quickly accepted the challenge and off they went, through rice paddies almost thigh deep in water, to the hamlet about two kilometers distant. To get there also involved a river crossing of the Kim Song. Some four hours later the patrol returned almost dragging the surgeon and his party. They were completely soaked and totally bedraggled from the heat and humidity. After moving into the center of the perimeter the party fell to the ground, and began stripping of their well soaked pants, boots and socks. There feet were wrinkled, red, and blistered (they were wearing regular combat boots vice jungle boots) and their skin had cracked and was bleeding. With a sheepish grin the Surgeon simply stated "Captain, you can rest assured I will no longer be questioning why so many men of the CAV are showing up at the 15th Med Hospital with trench foot anymore." We called for a helicopter which soon arrived and they flew back to Camp Radcliffe somewhat chagrined, but with a better understanding of the life of an infantryman in Vietnam during the rainy season.

The Company returned to regular business, running squad and platoon size patrols, in search of any enemy soldiers who had survived and were trying to evade and escape the area. The rest of the Battalion were doing the same in different locations within 3-5 kilometers of Bravo Company's main location in Gia Duc (1). Although no major contacts were made with the retreating enemy, caches were discovered resulting in a significant amount of captured equipment, medical supplies, rice and dead enemy soldiers who had been killed by the continued artillery and helicopter gunship strikes in the area or who had been severely wounded and left to die by their comrades. The 1967 New Year came in, but not with any celebrations. It was strictly a normal working day for us. Alpha Company, who had joined the Battalion in a search of the area to the south of us, captured 4 NVA/VC near where D Company had deployed on the 28th. They stated they had participated in the assault on LZ Bird, but were separated from their unit while withdrawing back to the north.

The New Year also saw all the Companies of the Battalion return to routine patrolling duties with squad, platoon, and company size units throughout Binh Dinh Province initially in the area surrounding Gia Duc and Hoi An to the south, then again moving into the mountains separating the Soui Ca and the Vinh Thanh Valleys in and around the same areas we had operated during Operation Crazy Horse.

On January 2nd B Company, while searching a hamlet southeast of Gia Duc near the river, captured a wounded NVA Lieutenant who had participated on the attack on LZ Bird and the fight in Gia Duc. The company had been augmented by an ARVN Airborne squad and as they moved through the village the ARVN leader walked over to a women villager, said something to her, then reached and ripped the front of her blouse. She was in fact a he and turned out to be the aforementioned NVA officer. He stated he was the commander of the 4th Company, 8th Battalion, 22nd NVA Regiment and that he had been wounded on the

28th and left behind to recuperate. He also said most of the survivors of the attack on LZ Bird and the action on the 28th of December had fled through the mountains to the vicinity of Van Hoi (1) and (3) hamlets, northwest of Gia Duc (1) and said most of the remaining elements of the Regiment had either been killed or captured. He also identified the Commander of the 8th Battalion as Nguyen Ahn Dung.

Several days later after intense patrolling in the mountainous area near Gia Duc and the villages in the low ground surrounding the river, the company discovered several caches of enemy equipment and supplies. On 4 January 1967 we discovered an even larger cache and killed one NVA soldier, wounded three and captured six enemy combatants. The next day the company uncovered yet another large cache of weapons and equipment, including a substantial quantity of rice. An enemy nurse was also captured carrying medical supplies. These caches were located in the mountains to the SW of Gia Duc. The other companies of the Battalion were having similar results as they scoured the mountainous terrain around and to the south of Gia Duc and Hoai An. In numerous instances the maneuver units found the bodies of NVA/VC who had been killed by artillery or gunships. On one search in the coastal plain misfortune again hit the company when Lt Frye, Sp4 Lloyd Jack and a young black soldier were all wounded when a booby trapped cluster bomblet was triggered. They were quickly evacuated by helicopter to 85th Evac Hospital in Qui Nhon. All survived the explosion, but were badly injured, enough so that all were evacuated eventually to hospitals in Japan, then stateside. I was able to visit all of them at the hospital before they left. Jack was the most seriously injured and although I feared for his life he pulled through. When I met with him he was covered from head to foot in bandages, except for his face and left arm. He immediately asked me to take a picture of him in his own words, "The folks back home will never believe this shit." Jack served as my RTO for several months prior to being wounded and had only returned to the 2nd Platoon 2-3 weeks prior to the incident. Lt John Lindsey replaced Frye as the 2nd Platoon Leader a few weeks later.

CHAPTER 29

FAMILIAR TERRITORY OR WAS IT

After a few days, with no additional contacts with either NVA or VC units or individuals, the Battalion operations were shifted south to the Crows Foot area in Binh Dinh Province, specifically the familiar mountainous terrain between the Soui Ca and Vinh Thanh Valleys where the Battalion was placed under the operational control (Opconned) to the 3rd Brigade, 25th Infantry Division who had been given control of all operations in the mountainous area. The Company initially moved to LZ Hammond for resupply and then air assaulted into LZ Meade (BR 788732), after spending several days at the LZ due to inclement weather which precluded air activity. Meade proved to be a dry hole with no enemy presence located in the area and on January 11th the Company then assaulted into LZ Snake (BR 622632), an area we had occupied during the latter phase of Operation Crazy Horse. Again, we ran into no enemy resistance as we patrolled the high ground overlooking the Vinh Thanh Valley, a former Viet Cong stronghold. Other units of the Battalion were inserted into familiar Landing Zones that had also been used during Crazy Horse. Alpha and Delta companies found an abandoned base camp several hundred meters south of LZ Horse capable of containing a sizeable enemy force and may have, in fact, done so during the operation in May and early June 1966.

The battalion as a whole only had a few minor skirmishes while searching the mountainous terrain between the two valleys. The significant contacts were on the 22nd when Alpha Company killed 6 VC, one who appeared to be of Chinese extraction. One member of Alpha Company was killed and two wounded during the encounter. On the 24th, Delta Company engaged an enemy unit 2 kilometers south of LZ Crater (BR 725618) or roughly 4 kilometers southeast of LZ Horse resulting in 13 Viet Cong killed with no friendly casualties. Two days later Bravo Company replaced Delta and killed 2 additional Viet Cong in the same general area.

On the 27th Battalion Forward was established at LZ Wedge, six kilometers southeast of LZ Horse and Bravo Company was inserted about two kilometers north of the forward CP in the same general area where Delta had had made contact a week prior. The following day tragedy struck Alpha Company when they discovered a US backpack in an abandoned hut. The Company Commander Captain John Titus, a West Point graduate was killed instantly when a booby trap exploded as he picked the pack up. Seven others were wounded, including the Platoon leader of the 4th Platoon. I believe the Company RTO later died of his wounds. The death of Titus was a shock to the Battalion as he was extremely well liked by his men and other members of the Battalion.

Fig 55. Captain John Titus, CO, A Company, 1/8th Cav

Bravo was ordered to link up with Alpha to assist, but while maneuvering towards them found several graves and a large cave complex filled with medical supplies. The cave had been recently occupied. A short distance to the south the company found an even larger cave, with an elevated sleeping area and wet clothing again indicating recent occupation. They also found a large stack of documents. A stream flowed through the cave and many fresh footprints were found on trails leading away from the area. It was apparent that the enemy occupying the complex had recently fled the area to avoid contact with the company. Two days later the company located a company size enemy bivouac area containing 30 huts near a stream. As they searched the area they came under fire from a possible security team resulting in PFC Gerald Maguire being killed and one other wounded in the encounter. One enemy soldier was also killed. We then returned to LZ Gavin for a short stay to provide security to the artillery battery still at this location.

CHAPTER 30

THE ROCK

The company closed out the month when we again air assaulted into the familiar mountains just west of the Soui Ca Valley while under operational control of the 1/39th Infantry/4th Infantry Division who had assumed operational control of the area. On landing the company moved up a finger ridge to the north along a wide, well used trail. We soon arrived at a large boulder which was bisected by the trail. The boulder was approximately 20 feet high. Villaronga called a halt and ordered myself, my RTO and seven others to take up positions just to the north of the boulder and hold this position until the company returned. He explained the company would continue up the trail to the crest move east then south into a draw, move parallel to the finger ridge we were on, make a thorough search, and then return to our location. They then moved out leaving us to dig in and await their return in about 4 hours. We settled in with some trepidation as the area we were to defend, should anything happen, sloped steeply on both sides of the trail leaving us little maneuver room if we needed it. We listened to his progress over the radio as he and the company moved along the route he had planned out.

Around 1600 hours the company made contact with a small enemy force while moving down the draw. After an exchange of fire the enemy fled into a cave complex about 5 kilometers southeast of LZ Crater. Attempts were made to talk the enemy out of the complex, but to no avail. A brief exchange of fire resulted in three NVA killed. SGT Daniel Herrando, the artillery recon Sergeant from the 2/19th Artillery, who had entered the cave in pursuit of the enemy force was fatally shot and all attempts to recover his body were met with a hail of fire.

Fig 56. SGT Daniel Herrando, Artillery Recon Sergeant, 2/19 Artillery

Villaronga, frustrated that Herrando entered the cave in pursuit of the enemy soldiers, then called for engineer support to assist in recovering the body of Herrando using CS (tear) gas to incapacitate the enemy force. He was informed they would be sent in the next morning.

My small element was then notified we would have to stay in position on the ridge for the night and when the body was recovered the company would then rejoin us. I was not a happy camper sitting on a heavily used trail with only our individual weapons and knowing enemy forces were in the area. Villaronga said not to worry, he would call in prepositioned artillery locations that we could adjust from should any enemy units move on the trail. He proceeded to do so. The first marking round hit about 150 yards north of our position. I asked him to drop the fire 50, which he did. Again it was right on target. I then asked he drop again and this time the round sent shrapnel into the boulder we were sitting near. One piece the size of a fist hit about a foot above my head and I immediately said, "that's close enough, should we need the fire, this is where I will adjust from." Franky it had scared the hell out of me and the men with me. Thank God we did not need it and the next day the company rejoined us before we moved back into the valley and then returned to LZ Gavin.

CHAPTER 31

CONTINUED OPERATIONS AND THE MOVE TO LZ ENGLISH

Alpha Company and the Battalion Forward Command Post was moved from LZ Crater to LZ Putter. Two days later B Company returned to operational control of the 1/8th at LZ Putter, less the 3rd Platoon, who was air lifted to LZ Meade. Meade as I recall was mainly a radio relay station between the Base Camp at Anh Khe and the South China Sea in the east. The 3rd Platoon would provide security for the signal company occupying the LZ. The company immediately began patrolling the area to the north and east of Putter. Little activity occurred during the next week. Delta Company found several caches but no enemy contact. Bravo had one contact during the period with no casualties on either side then joined the 3rd Platoon on LZ Meade before air assaulting into LZ Hook near the Con River, which flowed the length of the Vinh Thanh valley. Contact was made immediately with an unknown enemy size force resulting in 3 enemy KIA and possibly 3 more who were on the opposite bank of the river. At least two bodies floated down the swollen river precluding an accurate count.

Meanwhile the Division Forward CP was moved from LZ Hammond to LZ English approximately 45 kilometers to the north, near the town of Bong Son. English was located in the fertile Bong Son Plain, a rich rice growing area and to the west were the mountains surrounding the

Kim Song Valley and the Crows Feet area, havens for the 18th and 22nd NVA Regiments. I was placed in charge of rear area security as the large convoy departed Hammond heading north along Highway 1. Just before departure I and my two supply clerks, SGT Charles Allen and Sp4 Tom Silinsky, were approached by two US Army CID (Criminal Investigation Division) personnel who questioned us about a small jeep trailer that was near our area on Hammond. Knowing a former member of our company had acquired it through nefarious means some time in 1965 or early 1966 I played dumb and stated I did not know who it belonged to. I said it had been there when we arrived at Hammond in September 1966 and we assumed it belonged to an ARVN unit. I know the CID agents didn't believe me for an instant, but they had no proof that any of us had anything to do with the theft of the trailer. They finally stated they would take possession and return it to its rightful owner which, I presume, they did.

This delay; however, left us far behind the convoy which had already departed Hammond and was well on its way to English. I contacted the convoy commander and asked him to hold up so we could rejoin the convoy. His response was don't worry "we are moving slow so you should have no problem catching up with the convoy." We never did and made the dangerous drive up National Highway 1 (the notorious "Street without Joy" so named by author Bernard Falls in his book by the same name) in a jeep with only our three M-16 Rifles and a .45 pistol for protection. The latter part of our trip was after nightfall and in a steady rain. We later learned an ARVN Convoy following shortly behind us was ambushed as they moved through a small mountain pass on Highway 1. I never found out the results of the ambush, but on reaching English let the Captain in charge of the convoy know what I thought of him and his decision to leave us in no uncertain terms. Needless to say he did not like what I had to say and told me I could not talk to a superior officer in that manner. So I quickly ended the conversation with a big "F*** you A****** and if you ever do that to me again I will personally shoot your sorry ass" as I moved to join up with our forward trains position on the LZ. A few days later as the company continued operations, Lt Riffle was wounded by shrapnel in his left arm from a grenade thrown by an enemy soldier who was immediately taken under fire and killed. Riffle was evacuated, but several weeks later returned to duty.

Fig 57. Lt Roger Riffle, Platoon Leader 3rd Platoon, B Company

CHAPTER 32

LZ SAND AND THE BONG SONG PLAIN

On the 12th a change of mission for the Battalion occurred when Bravo Company was flown from LZ Hook in the upper Vinh Thanh Valley to LZ Sand (BR 840085) to the east of the An Lao Mountains overlooking the Bong Son Plain.

Bravo would secure the LZ for the Battalion Forward Command Post and A Battery, 2/19th Artillery. The LZ would become the Battalion's maneuver company's home for the next month or so with the companies rotating in and out to provide security for the HQs and supporting artillery. Numerous sightings of small NVA/VC units were noted as we moved into the LZ, but none engaged us as we landed on the LZ, which was about 300 feet above the surrounding rice paddies, hamlets, and villages. On landing we immediately began preparing fighting positions in anticipation of probing or outright attacks on the Fire Support Base and Battalion Forward CP. The Brigade's mission was now to deny the NVA/VC from collecting rice from this bountiful fertile rice producing area which was now being harvested and to destroy main force NVA and VC units who had populated the area for years. The Brigade CP was relocated to LZ Pony overlooking a major intersection where they would oversee operations in the Crows Foot and Bong Son plains area.

The companies of the Battalion over the next several weeks vigorously patrolled throughout the Bong Son plains area and in the Mountains to the West of LZ Sand with only limited enemy contact. Bravo Company in particular continued to secure the fire support base on LZ Sand while sending daily patrols through the surrounding villages and Hamlets to the south, east, and north of the LZ. Captain Villaronga in the meantime, knowing I would soon be reaching the end of my tour, decided to depart on R&R to meet his wife in Hawaii. I would take command of the Company in his absence. Although thankful for the chance to take command on the 21st of February, I also had some trepidation since I had less than a month left in country. My fears were well taken when a week later I received orders for the Company to air assault from LZ Sand into the mountains separating the Bong Son plains from the enemy controlled An Lao Valley. The mission was to sweep the area to the south of the selected landing zone and to locate and destroy any enemy forces we encountered. A secondary mission was to clear the area to the west of LZ Sand and prevent any possible attack from the high ground overlooking the FSB before moving to the south.

On March 5, 1967 at 11:00 hours the assembled company was picked up on LZ Sand and flown in a circuitous route before being delivered to the designated landing area in the mountainous terrain almost due west of the Fire Support Base. The landing went without a hitch and we encountered no opposition. After a quick search we began moving south. As I remember the day was sunny with little humidity and the movement South was without incident. As we moved along the high ground we could see for miles over the Bong Son plain all the way to the East China Sea. The view was magnificent until we observed a huge explosion which brought us back to reality. Over the command radio we heard the report that a US Reconnaissance Platoon working to the east were hit by a command detonated booby trapped explosive, thought to be a 500 pound bomb. The Platoon Leader and his RTO simply vanished in the massive explosion and several other men in the platoon had serious injuries. The incident caused all of us to again reflect that we were in a war zone and that it could happen to any us if not careful as we searched for the ever elusive enemy.

At that point I ordered the Company to take a break for lunch. We had accomplished about half of our mission, but still had to follow the ridge back down to the Bong Son plain where we were to set up a night defensive position and wait further instructions. Following the short break we again began moving south along the ridge which was now sloping down towards lower ground. Shortly thereafter the 2nd platoon, who was serving as the point platoon for the company notified me they were observing a group of NVA/VC soldiers in the open to the south. I moved up to the front of the column and saw 12-15 armed enemy soldiers moving quickly towards the high ground south of our position. It was obvious they had spotted us and were fleeing the area. I immediately asked Lt. Neal Laughy, the Artillery FO to bring fire on them, only to find out there were no artillery units positioned to fire at that particular grid. Now I really wanted out of the field. Here I was leading a company in an NVA/VC heavily populated area with no artillery for support. After a few expletives I ordered the Company to resume our march back to the valley but with cautioned concern since we had been seen, specifically be alert and be ready.

On reaching the area we had seen the enemy force we did a thorough search but found nothing. They had simply vanished. Moving to the east toward some small hamlets I received word the Command Chopper would be inbound shortly to pick me up for a briefing on our next day operation. As it was nearing 1800 hours I notified the platoon leaders and the 1st SGT to establish a Night Defensive Position while I met with the Battalion Staff at LZ Sand. I selected a position about 500 meters from a small hamlet and approximately 2.5 kilometers south of LZ Sand and the men immediately began digging in for the night. They didn't need any prompting since they knew there were enemy forces in the area. I on the other hand boarded the CC Copper and flew back to the LZ for a briefing on our mission for the following day.

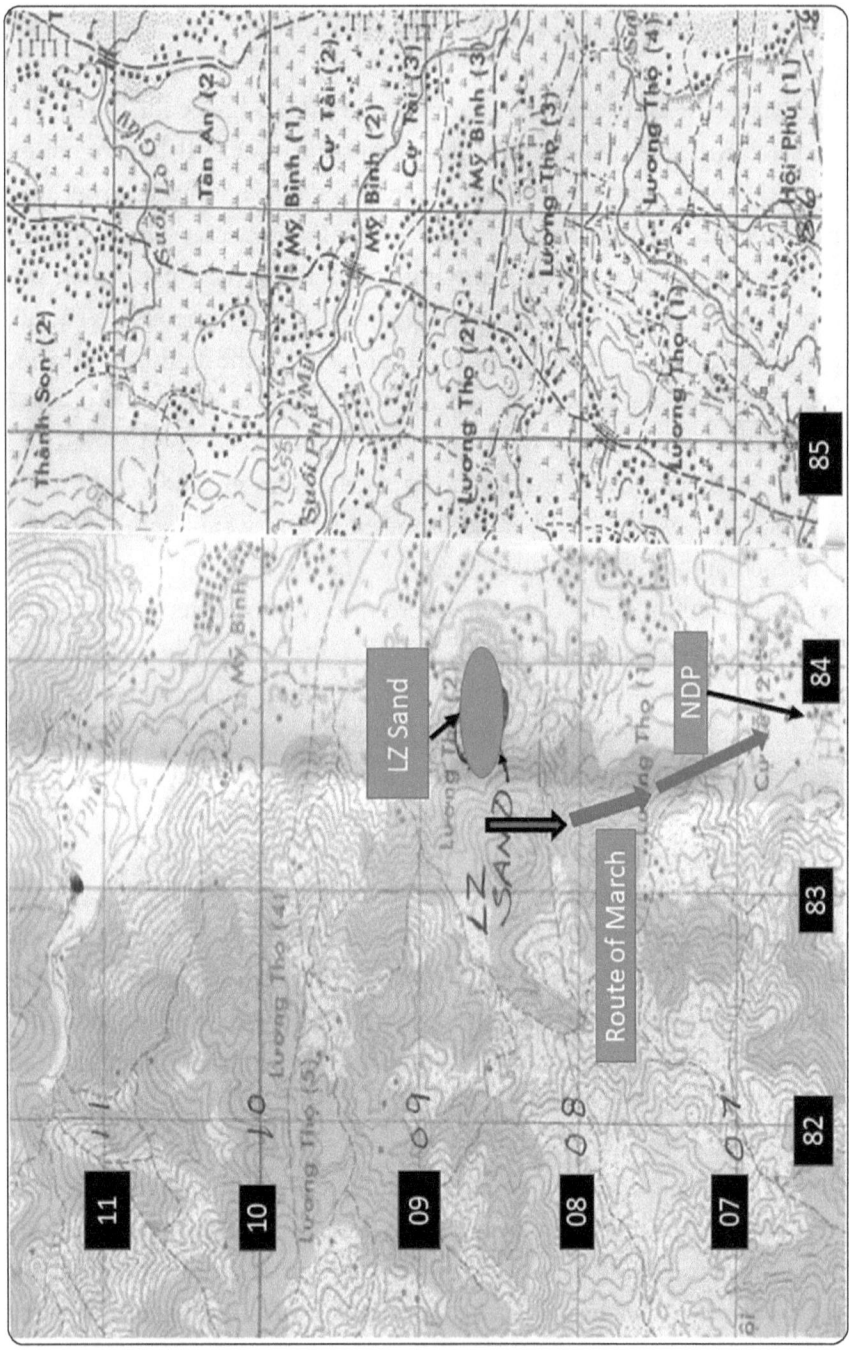

Fig 58. LZ Sand

And the Tears Flowed

On landing I reported to the Headquarters tent where I met with Lt Col McClure and his staff. After greeting me and some small chit chat he offered to give me command of a company in the Battalion if I would extend my tour for an additional six months. Although somewhat flattered I politely declined by pointing out to him every officer that had extended their tours in the Battalion had become casualties, and I did not like the odds, even though command of a company would have been a feather in my cap. He smiled and indicated he knew that I would turn him down. His staff then began the briefing and pointing to a map showed me what the company's mission was for the next day. Basically we were to continue moving to the east for approximately two kilometers and conduct searches of Hamlets/Villages along the route before turning north and returning to LZ Sand. Not a complicated mission although entering any Hamlet/Village was not without danger, especially in the Bong Son plains, an area long a hot bed for VC/NVA activities and their sympathizers. Col McClure then asked when CPT Villaronga was scheduled to return. I stated he had returned from R&R and was at Camp Radcliffe taking care of some personal business. He then asked when I was scheduled to depart Vietnam. I told him my DEROS as I understood it was March 16th. He looked shocked and asked, "Why in the hell are you still in the field." I responded I was waiting for the Company Commander to return and when he did I would then depart. He replied, "That will be first thing tomorrow morning, as soon as I can fly back to base camp and pick him up".

With that he, several of his staff, and I boarded the Command Chopper to drop me off at the Company's night defensive position. The pilot headed east for several miles then swung back to the west. As we flew over a village/hamlet (I believe Cu Le) about 500 meters east of the company's night location we began taking heavy ground fire and sustained several hits. Needless to say all I could think was "great we are about to be shot down on my last night in field." Thank God it didn't happen and we soon landed in the secure confines of the company perimeter. 1st SGT Craig met us as we landed and exclaimed to me "how in the hell did you get through all that fire. All we could see was a mass of fire reaching skyward and the chopper flying right through it" as the command ship lifted of and headed back to base camp at An Khe. I immediately summoned Lt Laughy, the Forward Observer, and told him to call in artillery and level the hamlet. Shortly thereafter a devastating barrage of 8" artillery fire hit the hamlet. Since we would be moving through this same hamlet in the morning we would then do a thorough search and perform a damage assessment.

After a quick breakfast, around six o'clock, the Company saddled up and began its movement to the east and toward the hamlet. On entering we saw almost total devastation. Virtually every home had been destroyed and palm trees were strewn everywhere. Since there were no inhabitants visible we then conducted a thorough search and rounded up about twenty to thirty villagers; old men, women and children, who they found hiding in bunkers. When questioned they stated a large group of NVA soldiers had been in the village for the past several days and were planning to conduct an attack on Landing Zone Sand the previous night, but thought the helicopter had spotted them. That is why they opened fire before fleeing into the mountains to the southwest. Our medics treated some minor injuries to the villagers and we then began moving to the east to continue our assigned mission.

Around 10:00 we received word to hold up, the Command Chopper was inbound to our location. We quickly formed a perimeter around a small dry rice paddy and the chopper landed. Captain Villaronga jumped out and Col McClure ordered me aboard. Villaronga protested and said I needed to brief him on the mission and what else had occurred during his absence. The Col said, "Ask the 1st SGT". With that I jumped aboard and, with a huge sigh of relief, was on my way back to Camp Radcliffe to begin my out processing. My year in Vietnam was finally drawing to a close.

CHAPTER 33

TWO IDIOTS

That evening I decided to celebrate so I headed for the Battalion Officer Club only to find it closed, which made sense since the entire Battalion was in the field. No sweat, I then headed for the 8th Engineer Club which was just down the road. Same scenario, they were in the field also. Now I headed to the Division Club about a mile away with the knowledge that no way in hell would that be closed. Lo and behold it was open and crowded.

While making my way to the bar I ran into Lt. Jim Murray whom I had been in the hospital with in Japan. Having completed his tour he was also heading home. We soon were downing beers celebrating the end of our tours. Around 9:00 Jim suggested we continue the rest of our celebration in the town of An Tuc. I asked how we could do that since there was a curfew in effect. He responded, "No sweat G.I. I have a pass that allows me to go into town anytime." With that we jumped in his jeep and off we went only to find everything in town was closed because of the curfew. No problem for us two idiots. We decided to go to Qui Nhon, some 50 miles to the east on the South China Sea. Without a second thought we headed down Highway 19, through the An Khe pass, and arrived in Qui Nhon just before 2200hrs. We quickly found a bar and settled in to enjoy a few more cool ones only to be told drink up, the bar closes at 11:00. We asked where else we could go and found out all bars closed at the same time. By now we realized we were facing a long ride back to An Khe. Even worse neither of us were armed and Highway 19 was one of the most dangerous roads in Vietnam to travel because of enemy activity. Nevertheless of we went. Just outside of town we happened to see an armed individual walking along the side of the highway. Stopping we realized he was a Republic of Korea (ROK) soldier who was trying to get back to his unit which was currently guarding the An Khe pass. We gladly told him to get in and we would drive him there. At least now we had one weapon with us. We dropped him at his unit in the pass and around 01:00 we finally arrived back at Base Camp. Jim and I just shook our heads as we looked at each other and bade each other farewell.

The next day I finished out processing and was told to report to the airfield the next morning for a flight to Pleiku, where I would then be processed for a flight back to the United States. This was accomplished and I soon boarded a Flying Tiger Airliner for the long flight to Travis AFB then to San Francisco International Airport for the flight home to Virginia. I arrived at Patrick Henry Airport in Newport News, Virginia, and was met by my family and friends for a tearful reunion. At long last my tour of duty was over and I was finally home with the family and friends I loved. Needless to say it had been a long and trying experience and one that I was glad to be over.

CHAPTER 34

CONCLUSION

Six days after I arrived home and serving as best man for my closest friend Wayne Hubbard, who was marrying my cousin Effie, I found myself admitted to McDonald Army Hospital at Fort Eustis, Virginia with life threatening viral hepatitis. The benefit of being so ill and stuck in the hospital was the girl of my dreams in high school came to visit me. Connie Russell had been my date at both the Junior and Senior Warwick High School proms, but while I was attending College she met and married a friend of mine. During her visit I found out she had separated from her husband and was currently living in Louisville, Kentucky with her parents and her two small sons, Leonard (Lonnie) and Randolph (Randy). She had returned to Virginia to visit her sister Patty and found out from her I was in the hospital at Ft Eustis. When she walked into the hospital room I knew I was not going to lose her again, and I didn't. In August immediately following her divorce we were married at the Ranger Chapel in Harmony Church, Fort Benning, Georgia and I adopted her two children who took my last name. A little over a year later we were blessed with another son, William Russell McCarron. We spent the better part of the next 50 years together with only two separations, another tour in Vietnam and one in the Republic of Korea, until her untimely death in late 2017 following lengthy illness. To this day I still miss her.

Fig 59. Connie and Me, Fort Benning, 1967

After nine weeks in the hospital I was finally released and returned to duty at Fort Benning, Georgia with the US Army Ranger Training Command. I also found out that three days after my departure from Vietnam, B Company, along with others of the Battalion and Brigade, engaged in a three day battle with the 22nd NVA Regiment some three kilometers Northeast of LZ Sand resulting in the company losing seven more members in the battle. Even though I was no longer in 'Nam nor with the Company, the death of these brave men whom I knew personally and had been with just a week before was still devastating. I had lost men whom I had lived with, ate with, and fought with. Their loss and the loss of the others I served with in Vietnam still to this day remains permanently burned into the darkest recesses of my mind and at times when I think back—the TEARS STILL FLOW.

IN MEMORIUM

This book is dedicated to the members of the 1st Battalion, 8th Cavalry Regiment, 1st Cavalry Division, and especially to those that paid the supreme sacrifice during my tour of duty with Bravo Company, 1st Battalion (ABN)/8th Cavalry Regiment. May they Rest in Eternal Peace.

May 21, 1966 – Operation Crazy Horse
Bravo Company

2nd Lt Robert H. Crum, Jr.

SGT Gerald D. Hoover

PFC Michael Cryar

SP4 Richard Lease

PFC Gerald E. Metcalf

SP4 Allen J. Ritter

PFC Michael E. DeVoe

PFC Angel E. Rodriguez

Charlie Company

SP4 David M. Jolley

SP4 Michael Vinnassa

June 24/25, 1966 – Operation Nathan Hale

SSG Bobby James

SSG Charles Edwards

Sp4 Adell Alston

Sp4 Johnny Hickey

December 28, 1966 – Gia Duc (1) Operation Thayer II
Bravo Company

1st LT Daniel Hennessy

1st LT Lamont Finch

PSG Lonnie Barber

CPL Douglas Hoag

SGT William Goode, SP4 Erineo Mendez, and SGT Robert Carter, B 1/8th Cav receive the Army Commendation Medal for Valor, Dec 66. Mendez was KIA, 28 Dec 66 in the An Lao Valley, Binh Dinh Province, RVN.

SP4 Erineo Mendez

SP4 Dennis Spahn

SP4 Eric Brannfors

PFC Richard Jacobs

PFC James Pawlak

PFC Carl Mercer

*PFC Walter Wonnacott (15th Med Bn assigned to B 1/8th)

Charlie Company

SP4 Alfredo Saenz

PFC Ronald Giroux

Delta Company

1SGT Joseph Moore

SP4 Stephan Finney

PFC Douglas Fenney

PFC Daniel Mobley

PFC Otto Baughman

Other B Company Soldiers Who Died 1966/Early 1967

SGT Oddie Hailey

SGT Donald Kramer

SGT Joe Jordon

SGT Robert Pinnell

SP4 Mark English

SP4 Robert Cartwright

SP4 Robert Bried

SP4 Charles Harmon

SP4 Jerry Golding

PFC Jan Grabowski

PFC Joseph Burnett

PFC Gerald Maguire

PFC Julio Martin-Torrez

PFC Phillip McNinch

PFC Robert Ocampo

When tomorrow starts without me
Don't think we're far apart
For every time you think of me
I'm right there in your heart.

Written by Chief Warrant Officer James E. Butler while serving in Vietnam and who ultimately was killed when the plane he was piloting crashed in Vinh Binh Province, Republic of Vietnam on March 20, 1970.

GLOSSARY OF TERMS

Airborne (ABN) – Designation given to those personnel or units who have been trained to parachute from aircraft and are awarded the Airborne wings and/or an airborne patch.

AIT – Advanced Individual Training which leads to award of a Military Occupational Specialty.

Air Assault – The movement of ground based forces by vertical take-off and landing aircraft-such as the helicopter-to directly engage enemy forces.

Air Mobile – A designation given to a unit who is deployed using transport helicopters.

Ambush – A surprise attack by troops lying in wait in a concealed position. Tactic used to engage and destroy enemy force usually after dark as they moved men and supplies.

Anti-Aircraft Artillery – Any weapon designed primarily to fire at aircraft, either helicopter or fixed wing.

AO – Area of Operations.

AOR – Area of Responsibility

ARA – Aerial Rocket Artillery

ARVN – Army of the Republic of Vietnam, the South Vietnamese Regular Army.

Ba Moui Ba – Vietnamese beer also called Biere 33. Another local beer was Biere LaRue.

Black Hats – Also known as pathfinders. Specially trained personnel who are sent to establish and control landing areas for airborne or assault units.

BOQ – Bachelor Officers Quarters. Living quarters for unmarried or separated officers.

Bunker – A fortified fighting position. In Vietnam usually made of logs or sandbags with overhead cover for protection.

CC – Command and Control helicopter used by the Battalion Commander.

CIDG – Civilian Irregular Defense Group. A military Program developed by the CIA to develop South Vietnamese irregular military units from indigenous ethnic-minority populations. Local forces organized to defend Hamlets and Villages within each Provincial District

CO – Commanding Officer

CP – Command Post

C Rations or Field Rations – C Ration was a prepared and canned wer combat ration issued to the military when fresh food was unavailable. A variety of meals came in several a small cans. They can be eaten cold or hot. Primary meal for troops when in the field.

Claymore Mine – A directional anti-personnel mine. Defensive weapon that is used mainly to protect friendly positions or in setting up ambushes to cover a wide area. Produces a fan shaped blast of ball bearing size pellets when fired.

Defensive Emplacements – Foxholes, bunkers, or defensive trenches.

Defilade – A position protected from observation of enemy forces

Finger Ridges – normally gentle sloping ridge leading from low ground to higher altitudes such as the military crest or top of the hill.

Flanking Movement – A military movement around an enemy forces side or Flank to achieve an advantageous position.

Forward Observer – An artillery officer or NCO who accompanies Infantry Units on the ground and calls in artillery for the unit if needed.

Hamlet – No legal definition but is usually a small cluster of huts/homes that when pulled together make up a village for political or defensive reasons.

H&I – Harassment and Interdiction Fire. Used by Artillery to fire on possible enemy avenues of approach or assembly areas.

Hooch – A small house or an improvised sleeping arrangement usually using ponchos.

Helicopter – An Aircraft that can take off and land vertically, to move in any direction, or to remain motionless. A primary means of transport for troops in Vietnam.

High Ground – In military terms it means if you control the higher ground it is to your advantage. The enemy must fight uphill to get to you.

Gun Ships – Helicopters armed with 14.5mm rockets, grenades, and machine guns.

KIA – Killed in Action.

LZ/PZ – Landing zone/Pick up Zone

M-16 – A family of automatic military rifles. The 5.62 caliber assault rifle was the primary rifle used by infantry personnel in Vietnam.

M-60 – the Machine Gun caliber 7.62mm was the primary crew served weapon used by infantry Companies in Vietnam. It was also mounted on helicopters, armed jeeps, trucks, etc.

M-79 – Is a single shot Grenade Launcher that fires a 40X46 grenade. Used by select individuals in an Infantry platoon.

M-72 – Light anti-tank weapon (LAW) is a light portable one shot anti –armor weapons system. Used by infantry unit to take out enemy bunkers.

Napalm – A highly inflammable sticky jelly used in incendiary devices such as bombs and flame throwers. Mainly delivered by bombs from aircraft.

NCO – Non-Commissioned Officer

NDP – Night Defensive Position

NVA – North Vietnamese Army

Nuoc Mam – A Vietnamese fish sauce used to dip vegetables and meat into. Also known as Nuoc Cham.

OCS – Officer Candidate School

PAVN – People's Army of North Vietnam

Piasters or Ps – Vietnamese money.

RA – Regular Army

RF/PF – Regular Forces/Provisional Forces.

RTO – Radio Telephone Operator.

TAOR – Tactical Area of Responsibility.

VC – Viet Cong. Communist Guerrillas.

VCC – Confirmed Viet Cong

VCS – Viet Cong Suspect

Victor Charlie – Name attached to the Viet Cong or Vietnamese Communist.

Village – A collection of scattered Vietnamese Hamlets.

WIA – Wounded in Action

XO – Executive Officer. The second in command of a military unit.

Reproduction of this document is prohibited unless specifically authorized by the author.

www.ingramcontent.com/pod-product-compliance
Lightning Source LLC
LaVergne TN
LVHW041705070526
838199LV00045B/1219